商务英语类专业规划教材

商 务 函 电

Business Correspondence

主　编　裴　沁
副主编　赵　丹　鲁　萌　李莞婷
　　　　苏晓静　刘　琴

武汉理工大学出版社
·武　汉·

内 容 提 要

全书共分为 11 章。第一章综述商务英语函电的要点,包括商务英语信函的特点、写作原则和要求、组成部分和书写格式,以及电邮和传真的格式。从第二章开始,按照实际外贸流程——建立业务关系、询盘、报盘、还盘和接受、订单及其履行、付款条件、包装、装运、保险、索赔及理赔来组织章节结构,每章的内容都包括业务简介、信函样例、写作步骤与技巧、有用的表达语句以及练习。

本书可以作为商务英语、外贸英语专业的本科、专科教材,也可供其他专业对该门课程有兴趣的学生使用。

图书在版编目(CIP)数据

商务函电/裴沁主编. —武汉:武汉理工大学出版社,2018.8
(商务英语类专业规划教材)
ISBN 978-7-5629-5841-3

Ⅰ.①商… Ⅱ.①裴… Ⅲ.①国际商务-英语-电报信函-写作-高等学校-教材 Ⅳ.①F740

中国版本图书馆 CIP 数据核字(2018)第 178105 号

项 目 负 责 人:雷 蕾(027-87523138)　　　　　责 任 编 辑:雷　蕾
责 任 校 对:向玉露　　　　　　　　　　　　　　封 面 设 计:芳华时代
出 版 发 行:武汉理工大学出版社
邮　　　　编:430070
网　　　　址:www.wutp.com.cn
经　　　　销:各地新华书店
印　　　　刷:武汉市天星美润设计印务有限公司
开　　　　本:787×1092　1/16
印　　　　张:8
字　　　　数:266 千字
版　　　　次:2018 年 8 月第 1 版
印　　　　次:2018 年 8 月第 1 次印刷
定　　　　价:19.00 元

凡使用本教材的教师,可通过 E-mail 索取教学参考资料。
E-mail:wutpcqx@163.com
本社购书热线电话:027-87384729　87664138　87165708(传真)
凡购本书,如有缺页、倒页、脱页等印装质量问题,请向出版社发行部调换。

前　言

　　商务函电作为国际商务活动中经常使用的联系方式,是开展对外贸易活动和其他相关商务活动的重要交流工具。目前许多高校的商务英语以及国际贸易等专业都把商务函电作为主干专业课程,旨在培养学生掌握外贸活动中各类商务信函写作的基础知识和必备技能,进而提升学生的外贸业务实际操作能力。为此,我们在总结多年教学实践经验,并参考借鉴国内外同类专业文献资料和商务英语实训软件的基础上,编写了此书。

　　全书共分为11章。第一章综述商务英语函电的要点,包括商务英语信函的特点、写作原则和要求、组成部分和书写格式,以及电邮和传真的格式。从第二章开始,按照实际外贸流程——建立业务关系、询盘、报盘、还盘和接受、订单及其履行、付款条件、包装、装运、保险、索赔及理赔来组织章节结构,每章的内容都包括业务简介、信函样例、写作步骤与技巧、有用的表达语句以及练习。

　　本书的特点是实用性强。每章的信函样例都参考借鉴了商务英语实训软件的相关案例资料,因而具有一定的典型性和实用性。信函样例后的写作步骤与技巧和有用的表达语句都是对各个要点的很好总结和归纳。因此,本书可以作为商务英语、外贸英语专业的本科、专科教材,也可供其他专业对该门课程有兴趣的学生使用。

　　本书由裴沁担任主编,负责全书的设计和统稿工作,并编写了第1章至第5章和第7章,赵丹编写了第9章和第11章,鲁萌编写了第10章,李莞婷编写了第6章,苏晓静编写了第8章,刘琴对书稿进行了补充和校对。

　　在本书的编写过程中参考过的国内外相关书籍和教材已列于参考文献中,在此向相关作者一并表示真诚的感谢。

　　由于编者的水平有限,书中难免有疏漏和不足之处,敬请各位专家和读者不吝赐教,批评指正。

编　者
2018 年 5 月

Contents

Chapter 1　Essentials for Business English Correspondence

Learning objectives

    To know about the meaning and functions of business English correspondence.

    To be familiar with writing principles of business English correspondence.

    To master the structure and format of business English correspondence.

    To be familiar with E-mails and faxes.

1.1　The Meaning and Functions of Business English Correspondence

Communication is of great importance in every aspect of modern society. Business communication is concerned with the successful exchange of messages that support the goal of buying and selling goods or services. Generally there are two popular forms of business communication, that is, spoken communication and written communication. Nowadays more and more people like to do business by sending faxes through a fax machine or even by sending E-mails through the Internet. Here the E-mail is just business correspondence sent or received on the web.

Actually, business correspondence refers to the business letters, cables, telexes, faxes and E-mails dealing in international trade, as well as in domestic trade, of course. According to various purposes, business correspondence has the following functions: to get action; to build goodwill; to furnish information. A good business letter can play a vital role in trade for increasing good relations and attracting customers. So it is of the utmost importance for the students who want to be engaged in international trade in future to learn how to keep in touch with firms or merchants abroad by correspondence and how to draft effective business letters. Next the following principles require our attention and understanding when writing them in international communication.

1.2　Writing Principles of Business English Correspondence

An effective business letter, just like a good advertising of a company, can deliver the positive image of the company to customers. In other words, a well-written business letter contributes to successful business. In order to writing a good and effective business letter, it is essential to master basic principles, which can be summed up into the 7Cs' principles, that is, conciseness, clearness, courtesy, consideration, completeness, correctness and concreteness.

1.2.1　Conciseness

Conciseness means the most complete content but the briefest expressions without sacrificing clarity or politeness. A good and effective business letter should be precise and to the point so as to save both the writer's and receiver's time. To achieve conciseness, the following rules are advisable:

• Try to keep sentences short and effective and avoid wordy expressions.

Wordy	Concise
We wish to express my hearty gratitude to you for your kind cooperation.	Thank you for your cooperation.
They attend the Shanghai Trade Fair for the purpose of finding a business partner.	They attend the Shanghai Trade Fair to find a business partner.

• Try to use modern English instead of out-of-date commercial jargons.

Out-of-date commercial jargons	Modern English
due to the fact that	as, because or since
express one's hearty gratitude to you for...	Thank you for...
It will be our constant aim...	We shall try...
We beg to thank you...	Thank you...
take into consideration	consider
Awaiting the favor of your early reply.	We shall be glad to hear from you soon.

• Avoid unnecessary repeat.

Some unnecessary repetition looks wordy as well as makes the readers uninteresting. For example:

We have begun to export our products to the foreign countries.

In this sentence, the word "export" just means "selling the products to foreign countries", so the adverbial "to the foreign countries" is unnecessary repetition of the word "export". The sentence should be rewritten like this: We have begun to export our products.

1.2.2　Clearness

Clearness is just the basic requirement in writing, because you must express yourself clearly to make sure the message conveys exactly what you want to say instead of being misunderstood. To achieve this, a writer should first have a clear idea of what he or she wants to convey in a letter to achieve one idea in a sentence, one topic in a paragraph and one matter in a letter, and then obey the following rules:

• Avoid using vague and ambiguous expressions.

The business letters never use some unclear or ambiguous words, since those words may make the receiver misunderstand the meaning of the letters. For example:

As to the steamers sailing from Shanghai to Seattle, we have bimonthly direct services.

Here the word "bimonthly" actually has two meanings, one of which is "twice a month" and the other of which is "once two months". Thus readers will feel puzzled about its meaning in this sentence. In order to achieve a clear and definite meaning, this sentence can be rewritten as the following:

We have two direct sailings every month from Shanghai to Seattle.

We have a direct sailing from Shanghai to Seattle every two months.

• Pay attention to the position of modifiers.

The same modifier will lead to different implication and function when it is put in different position of the sentence. For example:

We can supply 80 cartons of the item only.

We can supply only 80 cartons of the item.

In first sentence, "only" is used to modify "the item", referring that the supply is only this item, not others. But in second sentence, "only" is used to modify "80 cartons", referring that the quantity of the supply is only 80 cartons.

• Try to use necessary transitional expressions and focus on the rationality in logic.

When writing a business letter, it is important to pay attention to the rationality in logic and coherence. For example:

We wrote a letter. It was addressed to Mr. Henry. He is the sales manager.

The above three simple sentences are not coherent in meaning, because every sentence has its own meaning separately. Thus readers can't catch the main idea and understand what the writer will tell them at all. This problem will be solved if the whole sentence is rewritten like this: We wrote a letter to Mr. Henry, the sales manager.

1.2.3 Courtesy

Courtesy attaches the importance to writing business letters in order to leaving goodwill and strengthening business relations. It not only means politeness, but also means trading customers with heartfelt respect, friendly concern and considerate understanding. To achieve courtesy, the following suggestions are helpful:

• Avoid irritating or offensive expressions.

• Adopt the proper tone in negotiation.

• Answer letters promptly.

1.2.4 Consideration

Consideration refers to thoughtfulness, so it is a vital factor to create a good impression in writing. Try to put yourself in your receiver's place to greatly consider his or her requests, wishes, feelings and problems. To achieve this, the following tips are useful:

• Emphasize "You" attitude rather than "We" or "I" attitude.

The so-called "You" attitude refers to the receiver's attitude and "We" or "I" attitude means the writer's attitude. Compare the following pairs of expressions in the table:

"We" attitude	"You" attitude
We allow a 5% discount for cash payment.	You earn a 5% discount when you pay cash.
We are pleased to announce that...	You will be pleased to know that...

• Focus on the positive way instead of the negative way.

Generally the positive way is much better accepted than the negative way by customers when problems need to be solved in business activities. Compare the following pairs of expressions in the table:

Negative	Positive
We do not believe you will have cause for dissatisfaction.	We feel sure that you will be entirely satisfied.
Your order will be delayed for two weeks.	Your order will be shipped in two weeks.

1.2.5 Completeness

A good and effective business letter should contain all necessary information to the readers and answer all the questions and requirements put forward by the readers. Here completeness emphasizes that all the matters are stated or discussed, and all the questions are answered or explained. It is essential to check the message carefully before it is sent out. In order to verify the completeness of what you write, five "Ws" (who, what, where, when and why) and one "h" (how) should be used to check the writing purpose and content of the letter.

1.2.6 Correctness

Correctness means correct grammar, punctuation and spelling as well as proper tone and accurate style in language. To achieve this, the following tips are advisable:

• Choose true facts, accurate figures and exact terms in particular.

• Adopt the proper tone and avoid understate and overstate.

1.2.7 Concreteness

Each business letter always focuses on its specific purpose, so its writing should be vivid, specific and definite instead of vague, general and abstract, especially when giving a reply, solving a certain problem, making an offer, etc. To achieve this, the following tips are advisable:

• Know the specific writing purpose clearly.

• Use specific facts and figures.

• Choose vivid and convincing words.

Compare the following statements in the table:

Abstract	Concrete
We wish to confirm our fax dispatched yesterday.	We wish to confirm our fax dispatched on November 8, 2009.
We have drawn our sight draft on you as usual under your L/C.	We have drawn on you our sight draft No. 668 for the invoice amount, USD 890.00 under your L/C No. 226 issued by the Bank of China.

1.3 The Structure and Format of Business English Correspondence

1.3.1 The Structure of Business English Correspondence

A complete business letter generally consists of seven main and necessary parts and six additional and optional parts. Seven main parts are the letter-head, the date, the inside name and address, the salutation, the body of the letter, the complimentary close and the signature. Other optional parts are the reference, the attention line, the subject line, the enclosure, the carbon copy notation and the postscript.

1. The Letter-head

The letter-head is the beginning part in a letter and occupies the top of the first page. It is always designed verily in different business organizations. Now modern business firms prefer to use stationery with a printed letter-head.

The letter-head generally includes the following points: the sender's name (a company), its address and post code, telephone number, fax number, internet address / E-mail address, telex number, trademark or a brief slogan, etc.

It can be seen that the letter-head is usually used for identifying where the letter comes from and forming one's impression of the writer's company.

2. The Date

The date is a vital part of a business letter and it can never be mistaken or be forgotten in any situation. The format of the date differs from country to country. Generally the British style is day month year, and the American style is month day year. It is unwise to show the date in figures like 08/11/2009 or 11/08/2009, because figures may create confusion according to different styles.

Different from the position in a Chinese letter, the date in an English letter should be typed a few lines below the last line of the letter-head and above the inside name and address.

3. The Inside Name and Address

The inside name and address is the receiver's address and is typed at the left-hand margin two lines below the date. The information should be given in a way like this:

Receiver's name or his title

Company's name

Number of the house and name of the street

District, name of the town or city

State or province, ZIP code

Name of country

Such Courtesy titles as Mr. , Mrs. , Miss. or Ms. are usually used to address one person when the receiver is an individual. Use Ms. if you are not sure whether the lady whom you are writing is married or not. Sometimes the official position of the receiver should follow after the name if there is any official position of that person. For example:

Mr. Bobby Robert

Sales Manager

The Sunshine Co. Ltd.

56 Duke Street

London N. W. 4

England

When the receiver is a company, the inside name and address should be written as follows:

The Machine Engineering Co. Ltd.

256 Shengli Street

Wuhan 430000

China

"Messrs" is the plural form of "Mr. " and is only used for companies or firms, the name of which includes a personal element, like Messrs. MacDonald & Evans in the following example.

Messrs. MacDonald & Evans

46 South Street

London N. W. 4

England

4. The Salutation

The salutation is the polite beginning with a greeting to the receiver, so it varies according to different writer-receiver relations and the formality level of the letter.

Some common salutations are shown in the following table:

Salutation	People to be addressed
Dear Mr. ×××	Men
Dear Mrs. ×××	Women
Dear Miss. ×××	Unmarried women or girls
Dear Ms. ×××	Women, marital status unknown

Salutation	People to be addressed
Dear Dr. ×××	Physician, PH. D. holders
Dear Prof. ×××	Professor and any holder of a professional rank
Dear Sir(s) / Madam	No specific reference, formal
Gentlemen	No specific reference, formal
Ladies and Gentlemen	No specific reference, formal
To whom it may concern	You don't know yet who is the recipient
(Dear) First name only	Close friend, informal

5. The Body of the Letter

This part is the most important in a business letter, usually consisting of three paragraphs: the introductory paragraph to begin the letter; the middle paragraph to explore the details; the concluding paragraph to end the letter.

When writing the message, the writer should attach great importance to 7Cs' principles and keep the following tips in mind:

- Write simply, clearly, courteously, grammatically and to the point;
- Paragraph correctly, confining each paragraph to one topic;
- Type accurately and neatly.

6. The Complimentary Close

This part is just the polite ending to the receiver. Like the salutation, the complimentary close has various styles and should match that of the salutation. See the following table for details.

Situation	Salutation	Complimentary Close	Style
The name of the recipient is not known	Dear Sir Dear Madam Dear Sir / Madam Dear Sirs Gentlemen	Yours faithfully Faithfully yours Yours truly Truly yours	Very Formal
The name of the recipient is known	Dear Mr. Smith Dear Mrs. Smith Dear Ms. Smith Dear Miss. Smith Dear Mr. and Mrs. Smith	Yours sincerely Sincerely yours	Formal
The name of the recipient is known very well	Dear Bobby Dear Lucia	Yours sincerely Sincerely yours Best regards / Regards Best wishes	Informal

7. The Signature

The signature can indicate the authority of the letter and is generally placed two lines below the complimentary close. It usually includes a handwritten signature that is signed by hand and in ink, the typed-out name that is easily legible to the reader and the title or position. For example:

Yours sincerely,

The Overseas Co. , Ltd.

(Handwritten signature)

Lucia Smith

Personnel Director

8. The Reference

The reference is generally used as a useful indication for filing and makes it easier to file the letter and track it when required.

The reference may include a file name, departmental code or the initials of the signer followed by that of the typist of the letter and is often placed two lines below the letterhead. Generally "your ref." and "our ref." are two codes assigned to the letter by the recipient and sender. For example:

Our ref: 268 PY / pl (in an incoming letter)

Your ref: 268 PY / pl

Our ref: 864 SD / wd (in the reply to the incoming letter)

9. The Attention Line

The attention line is used when the writer want the letter attended by or directed to a specific person or department of a company. It is typed two lines above the salutation, underlined and centered over the letter. For example:

Attention: Manager of Training Department

10. The Subject Line

The subject line helps both the sender and receiver quickly identify the gist of the letter and is placed one line below the salutation. It is usually underlined and in boldface letters to call readers' attention easily. For example:

Re: Order No. 882

Subject: Your L/C No. 4489

11. The Enclosure

The enclosure indicates something else is enclosed or sent together with the letter. "Enclosure" or its abbreviation "Enc. ", "Encl. " is often used for one item enclosed, and "Enclosures" or its abbreviation "Encs. ", "Encls. " is often used for more than one item enclosed at least two lines below the signature at the left margin. For example:

Enclosure: Commercial Invoice

Encl. : Commercial Invoice

Encls. : as stated

12. The Carbon Copy Notation

When copies of the letter are sent to others, write c. c. below the signature or enclosure at the left margin. For example:

    c. c. Mr. G. Well

    c. c. The Osaka Trading Company

    13. The Postscript

The postscript is an afterthought, aiming at the drawing of the reader's attention to a point the writer wants to emphasize or something he or she forgets to mention. But in business letters a postscript is used for drawing the reader's attention to the emphasized point instead of adding the forgotten point by the writer. It is greatly advisable to rewrite the letter instead of using the postscript when the writer forgets to mention something important; otherwise it may imply that the writer has failed to plan the letter well. For example:

    P. S. The samples will be mailed to you tomorrow.

All in all, in a complete business letter, seven standard parts are necessary while the optional parts can be added or reduced according to specific situations. The following sample just presents the standard and optional parts of a complete business letter.

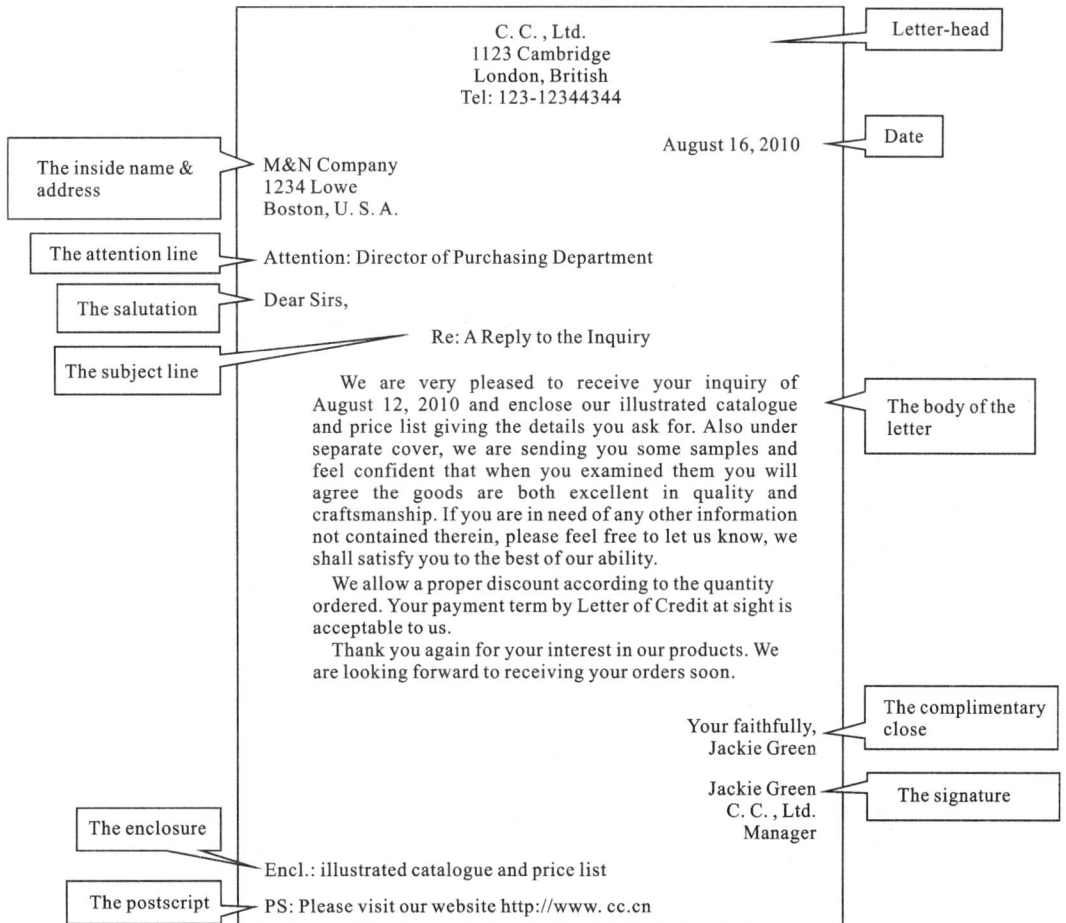

1.3.2 The Format of Business English Correspondence

Business letters belong to a formal writing style, so they definitely have the own forms. Generally speaking there are four popular forms listed as follows:

1. Full Block Form

In full block form, all typing lines, including those for the date, the inside name and address, the salutation, the subject heading and the complimentary close, begin at the left-hand with no indention in the letter.

The letter-head
The date
The inside name and address
———————————
———————————
The salutation
——————————————————————————————
——————————————————————————————
The complimentary close
The signature

2. Indented Form

The main feature in this style is that each line of the inside name and address should be indented 2-3 spaces, and the first line of each paragraph should be indented 3-5 spaces. This is a traditionally conservative format of layout.

The letter-head
The date
The inside name and address
———————————
———————————
———————————
The salutation
——————————————————————————————
——————————————————————————————
——————————————————————————————
The complimentary close
The signature

3. Semi-block Form with Indented Paragraphs

In this form, the inside name and address is typed in block form, but the paragraphs forming the body of the letter are all indented 3 or more spaces.

```
                              The letter-head

                                                         The date
The inside name and address

_____

_____

_____

The salutation

    _____

_____

    _____

_____

                                          The complimentary close

                                                     The signature
```

4. Modified Block Form

This form is similar to the semi-block form with indented paragraphs with one exception, namely, the first sentence in each paragraph is not indented completely.

```
                              The letter-head

                                                         The date
The inside name and address

_____

_____

_____

The salutation

_____

_____

_____

_____

                                          The complimentary close

                                                     The signature
```

1.4 E-mail and Fax

1.4.1 E-mail

An E-mail is a kind of letter which needs no paper, being sent to others by the Internet. It has some advantages such as arriving in time, being brief and cheap. In general, an E-mail has two big parts.

　　1. Heading

　　The heading includes the following aspects: from, to, date, subject, attn. (attention) and attachment.

　　2. Body

　　The layout of the body is like that of a private letter, including heading, salutation, body, close and signature. But sometimes it just has the parts of body and salutation, while the parts of close and signature are omitted.

From:
To:
Date:
Subject:
Attn. (attention):
Attachment:
Salutation
Body
Close
Signature

Sample

To: Joint company @ indeu. net

From: Litao@ yahoo. com. cn

Subject: about the production

Date: Dec. 10, 2017

Dear Manager,

　　One week has passed since you left for the United States. During this period of time, our production activities have been completely normal, and our output has increased by 1% on average in this week. What is more, the coal in urgent need for our production arrived yesterday afternoon just before the end of the work hours; so many people came to help unload the train. And I will tell you inspiring news that ABC company sent a mail the day before yesterday, asking for the renewal of the purchase contract for another three months and now all the procedures have been gone through.

　　Wish your visit a success.

Yours truly,

Li Tao

Production Department

1.4.2 Fax

A fax is a kind of letter which sends messages through the fax machine. The word of "fax" is the abbreviation of "facsimile". Like the E-mail, it has become one of the main means in modern business communications. Generally, a fax also consists of two parts.

1. Heading

The heading includes the following aspects: organization, address, tel., fax No., E-mail, to, from, date, attn. (attention), fax No., page(s) and re (regarding).

2. Body

The layout of the body is like that of a private letter, consisting of heading, salutation, body, close and signature.

Sample

Zhuhai Chemical Equipment Co., Ltd

Address: 36 Qinglu Rd.　Fax: 0756-4567886

Tel: 0756-4567889　E-mail: zce@ public. pta. net. cn

Telephone Message and Memo

Writing Tips

To: Guangzhou Industrial and Commercial Trade Company　　Attn: Mr. Wang

From: Mr. Zhang　　　　　　　　　Date: 2005218

Fax No. : 020-2346789　　　　　　　Page(s):1

Subject: Hope

Dear Mr. Wang,

　　The development of agricultural technology and equipment is playing an important role in our country's agriculture. Our company will participate in the exhibition of agrochemicals, agricultural technology and equipment, which will be held in Zhuhai next month.

　　We hope that we can take part in it with us, too. If so, we can exchange the technological information and cooperate in the trade in a better way.

Yours truly,

Zhang Lin

 **Words and phrases**

correspondence	函电
goodwill	良好关系
conciseness	简要、简洁
clearness	清楚
courtesy	礼貌
consideration	体谅
completeness	完整

correctness	正确
concreteness	具体
wordy	冗长的
Shanghai Trade Fair	上海交易会
ambiguous	有歧义的
steamer	货轮
rationality	合理
coherence	连贯
irritating	激怒的
offensive	冒犯的
punctuation	标点符号
abstract	抽象的
letter-head	信头
inside name and address	信内名称和地址
salutation	称呼
complimentary close	结尾敬语
signature	签名
Messrs.	先生[主要用作 Mr. 的复数，用于含有人名的公司名称前]
reference	编号
attention line	注意事项
subject line	主题
enclosure	附件
carbon copy notation	抄送
postscript	附言
full block form	齐头式
indention	缩进
indented form	缩进式
semi-block form with indented paragraphs	半齐头式
modified block form	改良齐头式
attachment	附件
abbreviation	缩写

1.5　Exercises

Ⅰ. Comprehensive Questions.

1. What are the basic principles of good business letters' writing?

2. What does promptness mean in the principle of courtesy?

3. What must we consider first before writing a business letter?

4. What are the main styles of business letters?

5. How can you write a good business letter?

II. Arrange the following information in a proper form of a business letter.

1. Sender's name: Tianjin Textiles Import and Export Corporation

2. Sender's address: 89 Xingfu Road, Tianjin, China

3. Sender's telephone: 86-022-23121431

4. Senders' fax: 86-022-23121432

5. Date: November 8, 2017

6. Receiver's name: The Pakistan Trading Company

7. Receiver's address: 15 Broad Street Karachi, Pakistan

8. Salutation: Dear Sirs

9. Subject line: ...

10. Message: ...

11. Complimentary close: ...

12. Signature: ...

Chapter 2　Establishing Business Relations

Learning objectives

To know about the importance of establishing business relations.

To be familiar with the channels of obtaining business information.

To master steps and procedures of writing letters of establishing business relations.

To master useful expressions used in letters of establishing business relations.

2.1　Brief Introduction

No clients, no business. Finding potential clients to establish business relations is a key and the first step for any company, because all transactions happen after establishing business relations, which is the base of starting and developing business. Good beginning is half success. Therefore, the importance of the first step cannot be ignored. As a seller, he has to find and persuade customers to buy his products or supply goods or services needed. Generally a company can get information of its prospective clients through the following advisable channels:

1. The data analysis

An enterprise can find potential customers by analyzing the relevant statistical data, directory data, newspaper data, etc. The statistical data refers to the statistical survey reports or materials from the authorizing departments or industry groups. The directory data refers to business directory, membership directory, directory of associations, Yellow Pages, company yearbook, etc. The newspaper data contains advertisements, financial information, industry trends and counterparts' activities from newspaper, periodicals or magazines.

2. The introduction from the third party

Here the third party refers to business connections or partners, banks at home and abroad, Councils for Promotion of International Trade, the Commercial Councilor's Office, the Chambers of Commerce or trade fairs at home and abroad.

3. Searching the Internet

The following websites are advisable for finding potential customers by searching the Internet:

(1) The main search engines, e. g. : Google, Baidu, etc.

(2) The industry websites.

(3) The company database, e. g. : THOMPSON.

(4) The directory websites.

(5) B2B websites.

After finding prospective clients from any of the above-mentioned channels, the first letter to establish business relations can be sent to the other party. The first letter is crucial for opening and enlarging market, because the first impression is very important. Generally speaking, this kind of letter should be simple, clear, cordial and skillful so as to reach the final aim successfully. Always use clear, simple and straightforward language and avoid poetic and artistic expressions, idioms, colloquialisms and slangs, which will confuse the receiver. The following are the specific sample letters from different perspectives.

2.2　Specimen Letters

 **Letter** 1

Dear Sirs,

　　We learned from the Commercial Counselor of our Embassy in Singapore that you deal in tablecloths.

　　We sell Chinese tablecloths. They are of good quality and have fine workmanship. Chinese tablecloths are very popular in Europe. We would like to work with you to market them in Canada.

　　We are sending you under separate cover by airmail a copy of the latest catalogue. Please let us know if there are any items which are of interest to you and we will send you quotations and samples.

　　We hope to hear from you soon.

Yours faithfully,

(Signature)

 **Notes**

1. Commercial Counselor：商务参赞处

2. deal in：经营；做……生意；交易

　　e. g. ：The company deals in both hardware and software.

　　　　这家公司既经营硬件，又经营软件。

3. tablecloth：n. 台布；桌布

4. workmanship：n. 工艺；手艺

　　e. g. ：This vase is a piece of exquisite workmanship.

　　　　这花瓶的工艺很精。

　　　　The problem may be due to poor workmanship.

　　　　问题可能出在拙劣的工艺上。

5. market：vt. 营销；销售

e. g. ：The company is marketing its new line of beauty products.

这家公司正在推销其新的美容产品系列。

market：*n.* 市场；行情

capital market 资本市场	market economy 市场经济
domestic market 国内市场	market competition 市场竞争
real estate market 房地产市场	market share 市场占有率
stock market 股票/证券市场	market demand 市场需求
international market 国际市场	market price 市价
home market 国内市场	market research 市场调查
financial market 金融市场	market development 市场发展；市场开发
on the market 上市；出售的	in the market (for) 在市场里；想买的

6. under separate cover:另函邮寄

7. catalogue：*n.* 目录

the latest catalogue 最新目录

an illustrated catalogue 图解目录

8. item：*n.* 商品（尤指一件商品）

9. quotation:*n.* 报价

quotation sheet 报价单；报价表

(to) give / send sb. a quotation 给某人报价

10. sample:*n.* 样品

e. g. ：We're giving away 2,000 free samples.

我们正在赠送 2000 件免费样品。

 **Letter** 2

Dear Sirs，

　　We owe your name and address to the Bank of China，Lagos Branch，through whom we have learnt you are exporters of Chinese textiles. Now we are interested in importing your Printed Shirting.

　　We would highly appreciate it if you would send us all necessary information so as to acquaint us with the material and workmanship of your supplies.

　　Your early reply will be highly appreciated.

Yours faithfully，

(Signature)

 **Notes**

1. We owe your name and address to...：承蒙……告知贵公司名称和地址

类似的表达方式如下：

(1)We have your name and address from...

(2)Your name and address have been introduced /recommended/given to us by...

（3）Through the courtesy of... /On the recommendation of... , we learn that...

（4）We are indebted to... for your name and address.

2. textiles：*n.* 纺织品

e. g. ：Exports in textiles, toys and plastics have shown signs of improving.

　　纺织品、玩具和塑料的出口已经显出改善的信号。

textile industry 纺织工业

textile fabric 织物；纺织布料

cotton textile 棉纺织品

3. Printed Shirting：印花布

4. We would highly appreciate it if you would... ；如贵方愿意……我方将不胜感激。

类似的表达方式如下：

（1）We would be highly appreciated if you would...

（2）We would be highly grateful if you would...

（3）We would be much obliged if you would...

5. acquaint：*vt.* 使熟悉；使认识；使了解

acquaint sb. with... ；acquaint sb. that... 使某人认识、熟悉或了解……

（sb. ）be/get acquainted with... 认识、熟悉或了解……

e. g. ：You will have to acquaint us with the details of products.

　　你们必须让我们了解产品详情。

　　We are well acquainted with the market condition in Asia.

　　我们对亚洲市场行情很了解。

6. material：*n.* 原材料（raw material）

7. supply：*n.* 供应；供应的商品；供应量

e. g. ：The market has to be fed with an endless supply of goods.

　　必须向市场提供源源不断的商品。

supply and demand 供应与需求

short supply 供不应求

supply chain 供应链；供给链；供需链

supply system 供应系统

8. Your early reply will be highly appreciated. 如蒙早日答复，不胜感激。

 **Letter** 3

Dear Sirs，

　　We got your address through your website www. cnart. com. cn.

　　We are an importer from Asia and have excellent connections with major dealers here of light industrial products. Please send us some information concerning such items and also the prices.

　　At the same time, if you expose your products at any fair in China, please let us know the name and date of it so that we may visit you.

We look forward to hearing from you soon.

Best Regards，

(Signature)

 **Notes**

1. We got your address through...：我方从……获悉贵方地址

2. ... have excellent connections with...：……与……有良好的联系

e. g.：We have excellent business connections with several overseas companies.

我方与许多海外公司有良好的业务联系。

3. dealer：经销商

a leading/major dealer 主要经销商

authorized dealer 授权经销商；认可交易商

franchised dealer 特许零售商；特约经销商

dealership 经销权，代理权

4. light industrial products：轻工业产品

5. concerning：*n.* 关于；就……而言

e. g.：I have a question concerning the Nobel Prize for Peace.

我想请问一个关于诺贝尔和平奖的问题。

6. expose：*v.* 展示；显示（show, display or exhibit）

e. g.：They want to expose their new product on the fair this year.

他们想在今年的展销会上展示新产品。

7. fair：*n.* 展览会；市集

commodity/trade fair 商品交易会/展销会

 **Letter** 4

Dear Sirs，

We owe your name and address to your branch in Nanjing，who has informed us that you are in the market for men's garments. We avail ourselves of this opportunity to write to you in the hope of establishing business relations with you.

We are handling both the import and export of garments. In order to acquaint you with our business lines，we enclose a copy of our Export List covering the goods you required at present.

It is our trade policy to trade with merchants of various countries on the basis of equality and benefit to exchange needed goods. We hope to promote，through mutual efforts，both trade and friendship.

We look forward to receiving your first order.

Yours faithfully，

(Signature)

 **Notes**

1. You are in the market for...; You want to buy...;贵方想购买……

2. We avail ourselves of this opportunity to write to you in the hope of establishing business relations with you. 我方借此良机,特此来函,望与你方建交。

3. handle:*v.* deal in 经营

4. garments:*n.* 服装

garment industry 制衣业;成衣业

garment factory 服装厂,成衣工厂

garment design 衣服设计

5. business lines：经营范围;业务范围

6. enclose:*v.* 附寄;附上

e. g.：we enclose a copy of our price list for you reference.

　　　我方附寄我方的价目表副本,供你方参考。

enclosed：附寄的;附上的

e. g.：Enclosed is our latest catalogue and price list for your reference.

　　　随信附寄的是我方最新目录和价目表,供你方参考。

enclosure:*n.* 附件

7. Export List:出口商品目录

8. covering：关于;涉及

9. trade with：make a deal with...,从事贸易;和……做贸易;与……做生意

e. g.：We thank you for your letter offering your services and should like to discuss the possibility of expanding trade with you.

　　　谢谢你方来函表示愿意提供服务,我方愿与你方就扩大贸易的可能性进行讨论。

10. on the basis of equality and benefit to exchange needed goods：在平等、互利、互换所需的基础上

2.3　Writing Steps and Tips

Based on the above specimen letters，some essential writing steps and tips about business letters for establishing business relations can be clearly and accurately sum up into the following points：

Writing steps	Examples of expressions
(1)The source of the writer's information 写信人的信息来源——如何获悉收信人的名称和地址	We have obtained your name and address from the Internet.
(2)The writer's intention 写信人的写作意图——想要建立业务关系	We are writing to you to establish long-term trade relations with you.

Writing steps	Examples of expressions
(3)Self-introduction 自我介绍——写信人的公司业务介绍	We are one of the largest... importers in our country and have handled... for about... years.
(4)The writer's hope or expectation 写信人的期望	Your early reply will be highly appreciated.

2.4 Useful Expressions on Establishing Business Relations

1. We have obtained your name and address from the Internet.

我方从网络上获悉贵方名称和地址。

2. We got the information from our sales department that you have desire to cooperate with our firm in marketing our silk products.

从我方销售部得知,贵方愿与我公司合作,销售我们的丝绸制品。

3. Our market survey showed that you are the largest exporter of cases and bags.

我方市场调查情况表明贵方是箱包的最大出口商。

4. Your firm has been kindly recommended to us by the Chamber of Commerce in Tianjin, China.

中国天津商会已把贵公司介绍给我们。

5. The purpose of this letter is to explore the possibilities of developing trade with you.

本信的目的是探索与你们发展贸易的可能性。

6. We are willing to establish business relations with your company on the basis of equality and mutual benefit.

我方愿与贵方在平等互利的基础上建立业务关系。

7. We are writing to you to establish long-term trade relations with you.

我方特来函,以期与贵方建立长期的业务关系。

8. We have the pleasure of introducing ourselves to you with the hope that we may have an opportunity of cooperating with you in your business extension.

我方有幸自荐,盼望能有机会与你们合作,扩大业务范围。

9. We are one of the largest... importers in our country and have handled various kinds of the products for about... years.

我方是我们国内……最大的进口商之一,已经营各类产品达……年。

10. We are exporters of long standing and high reputation, engaged in exportation of following items.

我们是声誉卓著的出口商,长期经营下列商品的出口业务。

11. We enjoy a good reputation globally in the field of machinery.

在制造行业领域,我公司享有良好的全球盛誉。

12. Our products have enjoyed popularity in Asian markets.

我方产品在亚洲市场上畅销。

13. To acquaint you with the new products we handle，we are sending you，by separate post，several booklets for your reference.

为了让贵方了解我方经营的新产品，兹另封邮寄一些宣传册供你方参考。

14. To give you a general idea of our products，we enclose a complete set of leaflets showing various ranges being handles by us with detailed specifications and means of packing.

为使贵方对我公司所经营的产品有一个总体了解，现随函寄上我公司经营产品的小册子一套，内有关于产品规格及包装条件的详细说明。

15. For our credit standing，please refer to the following bank：...

关于我方的信用状况，请咨询下列银行：……

16. We wish to establish friendly business relations with you to enjoy a share of mutually profitable business.

我方愿与你方建立友好业务关系，分享互利的交易。

17. We are willing to establish business relations with your firm on the basis of equality，mutual benefit and exchanging what one has for what one needs.

我方愿意在平等互利、互通有无的基础上与贵公司建立业务关系。

18. We are looking forward to your early reply.

盼早复。

19. Awaiting your favorable reply.

期盼佳音。

20. Your early reply will be highly appreciated.

如能早日回复，我方将不胜感激。

2.5　Exercises

Ⅰ. Multiple choices.

1. We would _____ very much if you send us some samples immediately.

　　A. appreciate　　　B. appreciate you　　　C. appreciate it　　　D. thank

2. Our products enjoy _____ in the world market.

　　A. good seller　　　B. great popularity　　　C. selling fast　　　D. most popular

3. We wish to introduce ourselves _____ a state-run company dealing _____ textiles.

　　A. as，with　　　B. for，in　　　C. with，with　　　D. as，in

4. We are sending you the samples _____ requested.

　　A. as　　　B. be　　　C. for　　　D. in

5. The booklet covers _____ wide range of products we deal in.

　　A. about　　　B. a　　　C. of　　　D. the

6. As the item _____ the scope of our business activities，we shall be pleased to es-

tablish business relations with you.

      A. falls within   B. lie within   C. be within   D. come under

7. We have your name and address _____ Canadian Commercial Bank who has informed us that you are in the market _____ canned meat.

      A. to，for   B. from，with   C. from，for   D. to，with

8. Your letter of October 10 sent to our Shanghai branch office has _____ to us for attention and reply.

      A. been passed through   B. passed on

      C. passed   D. been passed on

9. We are willing to enter into business relations with you on the _____ of equality and mutual benefit.

      A. base   B. bases   C. basis   D. based

10. When _____ an enquiry，you should enquire into quality specification，price, etc.

      A. offering   B. sends   C. giving   D. to make

Ⅱ. Translate the following terms and expressions.

1. owe one's name and address to...

2. the Chamber of Commerce

3. financial standing

4. under separate cover

5. for your reference

6. 商务参赞处

7. 插图目录

8. 享有盛誉

9. 业务范围

10. 建立业务关系

Ⅲ. Translate the following sentences into Chinese.

1. Specializing in the export of Chinese bicycles，we express our desire to trade with you in this line.

2. Your letter of Nov. 8 has been received and passed on to Beijing branch. They will reply directly as the items you enquired are handled by them.

3. Our handicrafts have met with a favor reception both at home and abroad.

4. As the items fall within the scope of our business，we shall be pleased to enter into direct business relations with you.

5. We write to introduce ourselves as exporters of silk products having many years' experience in this line.

6. In order to promote business between us，we are airmailing you samples under separate cover for your reference.

7. We wish to enter into negotiation with you with a view to introducing your special

lines in our market.

8. We enclose here a list of our import and export items for you as reference.

9. We shall be grateful if you will let us know whether you are interested in the above items.

10. It will be greatly appreciated if you will give us your cooperation.

Ⅳ. Translate the following sentences into English.

1. 为使你方对我们各种款式的手工艺品有初步的了解,今航寄我方一些目录和一些样品以供你方参考。

2. 鞋子出口业务属于我公司的经营范围。

3. 经行业协会推荐,我们很高兴得知贵公司的名称和地址。

4. 我公司丝绸在你地早已是热销商品。

5. 一收到你方具体询盘,我们马上寄送商品目录及样品。

6. 几个月前,我方有机会在上海世博会上看到贵方产品,对其品质和合理的价格印象极为深刻。

7. 据了解,贵公司是中国印花细布的潜在买主,而该商品正属于我方的业务经营范围。

8. 我们经营这类商品已经有二十多年的历史了。

9. 贵方想和我方建立业务关系的愿望与我们不谋而合。

10. 本公司专营电子产品出口业务,行销世界各国。

Ⅴ. Write a letter according to the following requirements.

浙江金海电器有限公司(Zhejiang Jinhai Electric Appliance Co. Ltd.)是一家大型的家用电风扇生产厂家,专注于家用电扇的研发、生产和营销达 10 年之久。在刚刚结束的广交会上,该公司推出了最新研发的电扇(型号:JH40-3B)。新研发的电扇在各个方面对原有产品进行了大幅的提升,并在产品质量和性能上经过了严格的测试,该新品意在面向欧美的中高端市场。在展会上,浙江金海电器有限公司的销售人员接待了来自加拿大 ICE 公司的客人,得知对方是加拿大本土主要的家电进口商之一,目前正在寻找高端电扇的供应商。

Writing requirements:

请以浙江金海电器有限公司的业务员 Jenny 的名义向加拿大 ICE 公司的采购经理 John 写一份开发信。开发信内容应包括:提及在广交会上的会面,向客人简要介绍己方公司及新品,附上新品资料,表达合作意向等。

Chapter 3   Enquiries and Replies

Learning objectives

To know about the meaning and categories of enquiries.

To master writing letters of making enquiries and replies.

To master the words and expressions related to letters of making enquiries and replies.

3.1   Brief Introduction

Generally buyers and sellers will start to negotiate on the terms of concluding the transactions when they find the opportunities of buying and selling in business. In international trade, negotiations generally include four major links of activities, that is, enquiry, offer, counteroffer and acceptance.

An enquiry is usually made by a buyer without engagement to get information about the goods to be ordered, such as price, catalogue, delivery date and other terms. Business negotiations usually begin with an enquiry by a buyer to a seller, enquiring about the terms of a transaction. Sometimes a seller can also make an enquiry to a buyer firstly showing his intention of selling certain goods to the latter.

Generally speaking, enquiries can be divided into general enquiries and specific enquiries. The enquirer in a general enquiry asks for general information, such as a catalogue, a price list, or a sample book, while in a specific enquiry, the enquirer focuses on the detailed information about the target goods or services, such as the specific quantities of the target goods, the discount, the terms of payment, the delivery date, etc.

The first enquiry, sent to a supplier whom you have not met previously, should begin by telling him how you know his name and address. Then some details of your own business will also be helpful for the supplier to make a decision.

In total, enquiries should be brief, specific, courteous and reasonable. The replies to enquiries should be prompt, courteous and helpful. In case the goods being enquired are not available at present, the supplier should inform the enquirer when they will be replenished and introduce some other similar products as substitutes so as to remain a good lasting business relation. An enquirer should state clearly his exact requirement to foreign suppliers, including prices, discounts, terms of payment, the time of delivery required, etc. There is no need for long and over-polite expressions, so in modern times using a printed enquiry form (figure 3-1) or providing an on-line enquiry system（figure 3-2）will be a quicker and more convenient choice.

发送询价单

深圳市意达特殊钢材有限公司
Shenzhen YiDa Special Steels Co.,Ltd

TEL：(86)755-28915911(50线)   FAX：(86)755-28912512

詢價單

等待我公司报价

编号	名 称	规 格	单位	数量	单价(元)	备 注
1	4140无缝钢管	外径23,内径17	KG	100	等待处理	不含税及运费
2						
3						
4						
5						
6						
7						
8						
9						
10						
11						
12						
13						
14						
15						

公司名称：深圳市意达特殊钢材有限公司　　联系人：周先生
网 址：www.yd-mouldsteel.com　　固定电话：0755-28915911-809
电子邮箱：yd@yd-mouldsteel.com　　联系手机：13823200919
地 址：深圳市龙岗区爱联嶂背工业区B栋　　传 真：0755-28912512
回复通知：☑ 站内通知 ☑ 邮件通知 yd@yd-mouldsteel.com　☐ 手机短信通知 13823200919
验证码：5981 5981

发送询价单   点击发送询价单

Figure 3-1

Figure 3-2

3.2   Specimen Letters

Letter 1   A first enquiry

May 22，2017

Dear Sirs，

We obtained the information of your company from the website of www. Alibaba. com. We are interested in the silk blouses you export and want to be informed of details of your various types including sizes，colors and prices.

We are large dealers in silk garments，having many years' experiences in this particular line. We are sure that there will be a good sale for silk blouses of good quality and moderate prices in our market.

When replying，please state terms of payment and discounts you would allow on purchases of quantities of over 200 dozen of individual items.

We look forward to your early reply.

Yours faithfully，

(Signature)

 **Notes**

1. We obtained the information of your company from...：从……获悉贵公司信息

2. be informed of...：得知；了解；获悉

e. g. ：People are informed of products and services by advertisements on TV.

人们通过电视广告了解到了各种产品和服务。

3. silk garments：丝织服装

4. a good sale：销路好

e. g. ：The market is advancing. Besides，our goods can always find a good sale.

行情上涨,而且我们的货物销路一直很好。

5. moderate price:适中的价格

actual price 实际价格   bottom price 最低价,底盘

competitive price 有竞争力的价格   favorable price 优惠价格

current price 市价,时价   cost price 成本价格

fair price 合理价格   base price 基价

6. terms of payment:payment terms,支付条件

7. discount:*n.* 折扣;贴现率

e. g. : They are often available at a discount.

它们经常可以以折扣价买到。

at a discount 打折扣;不受欢迎,没销路

special discount 特别折扣   extra discount 额外折扣

discount price 折扣价格   quantity discount 数量折扣,大批量折扣

cash discount 现金折扣   trade discount 商业折扣

purchase discount 购货折扣   discount interest 贴现利息

discount:*v.* 打折扣;贴现

e. g. : If you can discount your price by 15%, we are ready to take 600 cartons.

如果贵方价格能予以 8.5 折处理,我方乐于接受 600 箱。

8. on purchases of. . . :如购买……;在购买……

purchase:*n. /v.* 购买;采购

purchase price 买价,进货价格   purchase order 订购单,采购订单

purchase contract 购货合同   purchase cost 进货成本

material purchase 原材料/物料采购   purchase tax 购买税;消费品

make a purchase 购物   bulk purchase 大量采购,成批采购

purchase quantity 采购量   group purchase 团购

purchase discount 购货折扣   purchase requisition 请购单

 Letter 2   An enquiry from the importer

July 16, 2017

Dear Sirs,

We are glad to inform you that we are interested in your hand-made gloves in a variety of genuine leather. There is a steady demand here for gloves of high quality. Although sales are not particularly high, good prices can be obtained.

Will you please send us a copy of your catalogue for gloves, with details of your prices and terms of payment? We should find it most helpful if you could also supply samples of the various leather of which the gloves are made.

Looking forward to your early reply.

Yours sincerely,

Lucia

 **Notes**

1. hand-made：手工制作的

e. g. ：Because they're handmade, each one varies slightly.

　　　　因为它们是手工制作的,每一件都略有不同。

2. in a variety of...：各样式的；在各种各样的……

in a variety of ways / forms / circumstances

a wide variety of...：种种,多种多样的

3. genuine leather：真皮

4. There is a steady demand here for...：对……有稳定的市场需求

e. g. ：There is a steady demand here for high-class goods of this type, especially in the beautiful colors.

　　　　本国对此类高级货品有稳定的需求量,特别是色彩美丽的产品。

demand：n. 需求

a steady/strong/large/great demand for...：对……有稳定的/强烈的/大量的需求

in demand 受欢迎的；非常需要的；销路好；有需要

meet the demand 满足需要,满足要求；符合要求

market demand 市场需求　　supply and demand 供应与需求

customer demand 顾客需求　　consumer demand 消费/消费者的要求

domestic demand 国内/本地内部需求　　demand analysis 需求分析

strong demand 强烈要求；殷切需求　　actual demand 实际需求

5. Will you please send us...：请寄给我方……

6. We should find it most helpful if you could...：如贵方能……我方会觉得非常有益。

7. sample：n. 样品

e. g. ：The sample is for reference only.

　　　　此样品仅供参考。

free sample 免费样品　　standard sample 标准样品

small sample 小样本；小包货样　　test sample 试样

random sample 随机样品；随意取样　　representative sample 代表性样本

sample preparation 样品制备；样品加工　　sample data 样本数据

sample size 样本量；样本大小　　sample survey 抽样检查；样品鉴定

sample design 样品设计　　sample order 照样品订货；试购

sample room 样品间；样品陈列室　　a full range of sample 全套样品

sample：v. 取样,抽样

e. g. ：We sampled some goods to test their quality.

　　　　我们取一些产品做检验来检测其质量。

 **Letter** 3   **A specific enquiry**

January 16，2010

Dear Sirs，

We are in receipt of your samples with many thanks. We are satisfied with them. It would be highly appreciated if you could quote us your best price in USD per piece on CIF Montreal including 3% commission on your cotton blazers，Style No. BJ123. If your quotation is really reasonable and competitive，we will soon place a large order with you.

Meanwhile，please inform us other terms of transaction such as payment terms，package and insurance.

We are looking forward to receiving your immediate reply.

Yours sincerely，

Susan

 **Notes**

1. (be) in receipt of...:已收到······

e. g.：We are in receipt of your L/C covering 1,000 pairs of leather shoes.

我们已收到你方关于 1000 双皮鞋的信用证。

2. It would be highly appreciated if you could...:如能······将不甚感激。

3. quote:*v.* 报价

e. g.：No one can quote you a price lower than mine.

谁的报价也不会比我的报价更低。

quote us your best price 给我们报最优惠价

quotation:*n.* 报价

4. CIF：Cost，Insurance and Freight(insert named port of destination)，到岸价(成本、保险费加运费)

5. Montreal：蒙特利尔(加拿大东南部港口)

6. commission:*n.* 佣金

7. cotton blazers:棉质上衣

8. place a large order with...:向······大量订购

9. package:*n.* 包装

 **Letter** 4   **A specific enquiry**

August 8，2017

Dear Sirs，

We have just received an enquiry from one of our Japan client，who needs 10,000 metric tons of the captioned sugar and shall appreciated your quoting us your best price at the earlier date.

For your information, the quality required should be superior white crystal sugar packed in new gunny bags of 200 kgs each. Meanwhile, the goods should be surveyed by an independent surveyor as to their quality and weight before shipment. For this enquiry, the buyers will arrange shipping and insurance, therefore the price to be quoted by you should be on an FAS Dalian basis.

As there is a critical shortage of sugar in Japan, the goods should be ready for shipment as early as possible. Please be assured that if your price is acceptable, we will place an order with you right away.

Your early reply to this enquiry is requested.

Faithfully yours,

Susan

 **Notes**

1. captioned：*adj.* 标题下的；标题所说的

captioned order 标题所述订单

captioned goods 标题项下的货物

e. g.：We thank you for your enquiry list No. 228 and enclose our quotation No. 145 for the captioned goods.

感谢贵方第 228 号询价单，现随函附寄我方第 145 号标题项下的货物的报价。

2. superior：*adj.* 较高的，优良的，上乘的

superior goods 优等物品

superior quality 优质，上等品；高级货品

3. packed in：用……包装

e. g.：As requested, the shirts will be packed in waterproof material.

衬衫将按照要求用防水材料包装。

4. gunny bags：粗黄麻袋

5. survey：*v.* 检验；调查

e. g.：The products have been surveyed.

所有的产品均通过了检验。

survey：*n.* 调查；勘测

e. g.：I suggested they do some experiments, or at least a survey.

我建议他们做一些实验，或至少做一项调查。

survey report 检验报告　questionnaire survey 问卷调查

market survey 市场调查　survey result 调查结果

sample survey 抽样检查　detailed survey 详细调查

survey method 调查法　make a survey 做调查

surveyor：*n.* 检验员；测量员

6. FAS：Free Alongside Ship,船边交货价格,国际贸易术语之一。

船边交货(……指定装运港)是指卖方在指定的装运港将货物交到船边,即完成交货。买

方必须承担自那时起货物灭失或损坏的一切风险。

7. There is a critical shortage of/for... :……严重短缺

e. g：We already face a critical shortage of health-care personnel.

我们的卫生保健人力早已面临极度匮缺的局面。

8. be ready for shipment：备妥待运

e. g. ：The goods are being prepared for immediate delivery and will be ready for shipment tomorrow.

该货可以立即交付，准备明日装船。

9. Please be assured that... :请放心……

e. g. ：Please be assured that we will look into the matter.

请放心，我们会调查此事的。

 Letter 5　A favorable reply

June 22th，2017

Dear Sirs，

We are very pleased to receive your enquiry of June 20th and thank you for your interest in our products.

A copy of our illustrated export catalogue will be sent to you today，together with a range of samples of the various leathers used in the manufacture of our gloves and shoes. We think the colors will be just what you want for the fashionable trade，and the beauty and elegance of our designs，coupled with the superb workmanship，should appeal to the discriminating buyers.

Our representative，Mr. Black，will be in London next week and will be pleased to call on you with a full range of samples of our hand-made lines. He is authorized to discuss the terms of an order with you or to negotiate a contract.

We look forward to receiving an order from you.

Yours faithfully，

Lisa

 **Notes**

1. illustrated export catalogue：出口商品的图解目录

2. a range of... :一系列

3. the fashionable trade：（一次）时尚的买卖

4. the beauty and elegance of our designs：我方精美、优雅的设计

5. couple with：与……相结合，伴随，加上

6. superb workmanship：工艺高超、技艺精细

e. g. ：They are beautifully designed，of superb workmanship and unique in style.

它们设计精美、工艺高超、风格独特。

7. appeal to（sb. ）：吸引某人，对……有吸引力

8. discriminating buyers:挑剔的买主,识货的消费者

9. ... will be pleased to call on you with a full range of samples of our hand-made lines.

……将很乐意拜访您,并且带去我公司全部手工制作系列产品的样品。

10. authorize:*v.* 授权,委派

authorize sb. to do sth. 授权某人做某事

 **Letter** 6   **An unfavorable reply**

Dear Sirs,

    We were very pleased to receive your letter enquiring for our woolen sweaters.

    However, we regret to inform you that we are not in a position to cover your need for woolen sweaters. Once our supplies are replenished, we shall be pleased to revert to this matter.

    Looking forward to your more enquiries.

Yours sincerely,

Michael

Notes

1. enquire:*v.* (= inquire) 询价

enquire for 询购某物

e. g. : Thank you for your E-mail enquiring for walnut meat.

    感谢贵方来函询购核桃仁。

enquire about 询问……的情况

e. g. : I'd like to enquire about flights to New York.

    我想询问飞往纽约的航班的信息。

enquire into 调查,了解

e. g. : It is our duty to enquire into this matter thoroughly.

    我们有责任全面彻查此事。

enquiry:*n.* 询价,询价单

first enquiry 首次询价

general enquiry 一般询价

specific enquiry 具体询价

2. be in a position to do sth. : = be able to do sth. ,能够,能够做……

3. cover your need for... :满足贵方对……的需求

4. Once our supplies are replenished, we shall be pleased to revert to this matter.

    一旦我们的货物供应得到补充,我们将很高兴地回复这个问题。

replenish:*v.* 补货;补充;再加满

e. g. : Your body needs food to replenish its energy.

    你的身体需要食物补充能量。

replenish the stock 补充库存

5. revert to sth. : reply,回复,答复

3.3　Writing Steps and Tips

Based on the above specimen letters, some essential writing steps and tips about business letters for enquiries can be clearly and accurately summed up into the following points:

Writing steps	Examples of expressions
(1)Stating the source of the information (first enquiry) 表明信息来源(仅用于首次征询)	We obtained the information of your company from…
(2)Stating the goods wanting to buy directly 表明购买意向,即直接表明想要购买的商品	We are interested in… We are regular buyers of… We are considering the purchase of… Our lines are mainly…
(3)Asking for the catalogues, price lists, samples, etc. 做出询价,如询问商品目录、价目表、样品等	We would like to receive a copy of your latest catalogue and details of your prices and terms of payment, together with samples.
(4)Emphasizing the price quoted should be reasonable & competitive 强调对方所报价格需合理并具有竞争力	Provided prices are right. If your prices quoted are competitive, we will…
(5)Enquiring the discount, terms of payment and delivery date required 进一步询问折扣、支付条件、交货期等	We would like to know if you allow discounts.
(6)Showing the possibility of ordering the goods 表明订购商品的可能性	Please be assured that if your price is acceptable, we will place an order with you right away.

3.4　Useful Expressions on Enquiries and Replies

1. We have seen your advertisement in China Daily and shall be grateful if you will send us details of iron nails.

我们在中国日报上看到你们的广告,敬请告知有关铁钉的详细情况。

2. We are thinking of getting a supply of beans. Please send us your best offer indicating origin, packing, detailed specifications, quantity available and earliest time of shipment.

我们拟购蚕豆,请报最低价,说明原产地、包装、详细规格、可供数量和最早交货期。

3. As we are in the market for Men's Leather Gloves, we should be glad if you would send us your best offer.

我方想购买男士皮手套,贵方如能报给我方你们的优惠价,我方将非常高兴。

4. We are desirous of your lowest quotations for sewing machine.

我们想要你方缝纫机的最低报价。

5. When quoting, please state terms of payment and time of delivery.

报价时,请说明付款条件和交货时间。

6. We shall be pleased if you will furnish us with your lowest quotation for the following goods.

如果贵方为我方提供下列产品的最低报价,我们将会很高兴。

7. If you supply goods of the type and quality required, we may place regular orders in large quantities.

如能供应所需商品品种和质量,我方将定期大量购货。

8. We are on the look-out for the following items and should be appreciated if you would send samples of the same.

我方想求购下列产品,如贵公司能寄来其样品,我方将非常感激。

9. As the booklets you sent us were badly damaged in the mail, we would like you to mail us some more.

贵方的产品简介小册子在邮寄过程中已完全损坏,希望贵方能再多寄些来。

10. If the prices quoted are competitive and the quality up to standard, we will place orders on a regular basis.

如果贵方报价有竞争力,而且产品质量达标,我方将长期订购。

11. Please send us your latest catalogue with your best CIF London prices. We will also appreciate your telling us the approximate weight of each article.

请寄附有最优惠伦敦到岸价的最新商品目录,并告知每件货物的大约重量。

12. We regularly buy... and would like to know what you have to offer.

我方定期购买……并且想知道贵公司的报价如何。

13. We welcome your enquiry of December 6, 2017 and thank you for your interest in our products.

欢迎贵方 2017 年 12 月 6 日的询盘,并感谢贵方对我方产品的兴趣。

14. The enclosed price list and illustrated catalogue will provide you with the details of the various types you are most interested in.

所附价格单和图解目录将给贵方提供有关最感兴趣的型号的具体情况。

15. We should be much obliged if you could quote us the best CIFC 5% Shanghai and indicate the respective quantities and various sizes that you could supply for prompt shipment.

如果贵公司能给我方上海到岸价和 5% 的佣金的报盘,并说明能够提供马上装运货物的各自数量和各种规格,我们将不胜感激。

16. With regard to your enquiry for sewing machines, we wish to give the following in reply.

关于你方缝纫机的询盘,我方愿作如下答复。

17. In reply to your enquiry of July 16, we are sending you herewith our quotation together with various samples of leather boots closely resembling to what you want.

应贵方 7 月 16 日来函询问,现寄上我方的报价和几双式样不同的与贵方要求相近的皮靴样品。

18. We have much pleasure in enclosing a quotation sheet for our products and trust that their high quality will induce you to place a trial order.

我方非常高兴寄上产品报价单,我方相信我们的产品质量会促使贵方试订。

19. We trust you will give this enquiry your immediate attention and let us have your reply at an early date.

我方相信贵方会对此询盘予以重视并及早回复。

20. We hope that your prices will be favorable and that business will materialize to our mutual advantage.

我方希望贵方价格是优惠的,并且希望此笔交易会对双方都有利。

3.5   Exercises

Ⅰ. Multiple choices.

1. Will you please send us your prices for the items _____ below?

    A. listing   B. listed   C. being listed   D. to list

2. If the prices are _____, we trust important business can materialize.

    A. on the line   B. in line   C. in the line   D. on line

3. There is a steady demand in America _____ leather gloves _____ high quality.

    A at, with   B. in, of   C. for, of   D. for, with

4. _____ your enquiry No. 789, we are sending you a catalog and a sample for your reference.

    A. As   B. About   C. According   D. As per

5. If you are interested, we will send you some samples _____ charge.

    A. free of   B. with   C. within   D. for

6. The letter we sent last week is an enquiry _____ "Little Swan" automatic washing machine.

    A. on   B. for   C. within   D. as

7. If your prices are competitive, we are confident _____ the goods in great quantities in this market.

    A. to sell   B. in being sold   C. in selling   D. to be selling

8. They found an opportunity to purchase six _____ leather boots.

    A. thousands of pair   B. thousands pairs

    C. thousand pair of   D. thousand pairs of

9. As we are one of the leading importers in this line, we are _____ to handle large quantities.

    A. on a position   B. in a position   C. at a position   D. of a position

10. We enquire _____ Chinese Tea available _____ export.

    A. for, for   B. for, of   C. of, about   D. to, for

Ⅱ. Translate the following terms and expressions.

1. special discount

2. be in a position to. . .

3. terms of payment

4. replenish

5. place an order

6. 询盘

7. 优惠价格

8. 佣金

9. 交货期

10. 稳定的需求

Ⅲ. Translate the following sentences into English.

1. 我方对进口你方产品很有兴趣,如有可能请向我方提供目录、价格单和样品。

2. 如能对下列产品报最低价,我方将不胜感激。

3. 倘若价格有竞争性,我方已有现成买主,相信能大批量订货。(ready buyers)

4. 我方想大量购买各种型号的铁钉,请报每公吨新加坡到岸价。

5. 从贵方 9 月 18 日来函中,我方很高兴得悉贵方对我方新型彩电感兴趣。

6. 我方想知道订货超过一千打,贵方能给多少折扣。

7. 报价时,请说明付款条件和交货时间。

8. 现附寄最新目录和价格表,上面有贵方要求了解的详细情况。

Ⅳ. Translate the following sentences into Chinese.

1. As we are in the market for women's leather boots, we should be pleased if you would send us your best quotation.

2. Would you please tell us the price of these electric heaters so as to help us make the decision?

3. We would appreciate your sending us an up-to-date pricelist for building materials.

4. We are interested in motorcycles in various sizes and please send us a copy of your illustrated catalogue with details of the prices and terms of payment.

5. Enquiries for carpets are getting more numerous.

6. We shall be glad if you will quote us the best discount for cash for this quantity.

7. We enclose our quotation sheet against your inquiry No. 28 and look forward to your confirmation.

8. We regret that the goods you enquire about are not available.

Ⅴ. Writing practice.

Draft a letter according to the following points:

1. MODA Fashions plc. write to Armstrong Knitters plc.

2. They state that they are in the market for large quantities of ladies' tights.

3. They request samples in fashionable designs and ask for a discount for a large order of 400 dozen.

Chapter 4   Quotations or Offers

Learning objectives

To know about the meaning and categories of offers.

To distinguish firm offers and non-firm offers.

To master writing letters of quotations or offers.

To master basic expressions of writing letters of quotations or offers.

4.1   Brief Introduction

A quotation (报价) refers that buyers or sellers state some transaction terms about supplying goods to another party concerned. It is usually sent by the seller after the receipt of an enquiry. So, to some extent, we can say, a quotation is just equal to a reply to an enquiry. But sometimes a quotation can be sent voluntarily without an enquiry.

A satisfactory quotation will include the following points:

a. An expression of thanks for the enquiry (in the beginning).

b. Details of prices, discounts and terms of payment.

c. A statement or clear indication of what the prices cover.

d. An undertaking as to date of delivery or time of shipment.

e. The period for which the quotation is valid.

f. An expression of hope that the quotation will be accepted (in the end).

An offer (报盘) includes a firm offer and a non-firm offer. A firm offer is a promise to sell goods at a stated price, usually within a stated period of time. When the seller promises to sell goods at a stated price within a stated period of time, a firm offer can be made. An offer should include complete business terms (交易条件) and the validity (有效期). It will include the following points:

a. An expression of thanks for the enquiry, if any.

b. Name of commodities, quality, quantity, and specifications.

c. Details of prices, terms of payment, commission, or discounts, if any.

d. Packing and date of delivery.

e. The validity of the offer.

A quotation is not legally binding as a firm offer if the seller later decides not to sell. That's to say, if the seller later decides not to sell the goods, he can withdraw or cancel the quotation within its validity.

A quotation may have several different ways. The seller can give a price to the buyer for reference. He also can send a false quotation to negotiate with the buyer or send a true quotation as a suggestion of concluding a contract. Usually, to get an active position in business trade, the seller always sends a false quotation. Several expressions about a false quotation (or a non-firm offer) as follows:

a. This quotation is subject to our final confirmation. 该报价以我方最后确认为准。

b. This quotation is subject to the goods being unsold. 该报价以商品未售出为准。

Unlike a quotation, a firm offer can't be withdrawn by the seller within its validity. Only the buyer has a choice to accept or reject or counter-offer during the validity period. To get an active position, the seller always has additional conditions when making a firm offer as follows:

a. This offer is valid/open/firm for... days. 该报盘只在……天内有效。

b. This offer is subject to your reply here (or reaching us) by 5:00 p. m. , our time, April 14th. 该盘以贵方于 4 月 14 日我地时间下午 5 点复到为有效。

Generally, there are the following basic requirements when writing a letter of offer:

(1) Reply to one's enquiry in time, clearly and correctly.

(2) Include all terms of trade.

(3) Clarify it is a firm or non-firm offer.

(4) Introduce the advantages of commodities.

4.2 Specimen Letters

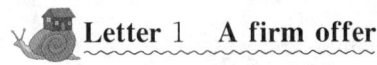 **Letter 1   A firm offer**

> June 20, 2017
>
> Dear Sirs,
>
> Thank you for your enquiry dated June 18. As requested, we are airmailing you, by separate post, one catalogue and three sample books for our Australian Royal wool blankets. We hope they will reach you in due course and will help you in making your selection.
>
> We are pleased to make the following offer, subject to your reply reaching us by 5 p. m. our time, Thursday, July 17, as follows:
>
> Article: Australian Royal wool blankets.
>
> Art. No. : 568239.
>
> Quantity: 8,000 pieces.
>
> Packing: standard export wooden case.
>
> Price: USD 79. 00 per piece CIFC 3% Seattle.
>
> Shipment: 7 days after receipt of the order.

Payment：by confirmed，irrevocable L/C payable by draft at sight to be opened 30 days before the time of shipment.

We look forward to receiving your trial order.

Yours faithfully,

(Signature)

 **Notes**

1. as requested：应贵方要求，根据贵方要求

e. g. ：As requested，we enclosed our catalogue and price list.

应贵方要求，我方随函附寄目录和价格表。

2. airmail：*v.* to send or transport by airmail，航空邮寄

3. by separate post：另邮

4. We hope they will reach you in due course and will help you in making your selection. 我方希望这些商品能准时送到贵方以供选择。

in due course：在适当的时候

5. We are pleased to make the following offer，subject to your reply reaching us by 5 p. m. our time，Thursday，July 17，as follows. 现乐意报盘如下，此报盘以我方时间 7 月 17 日收到贵方答复为有效。

(1)pleased：*adj.* 愉快的，乐意的，高兴的，满意的

be pleased/glad/happy to do sth. 乐于做某事

pleasure：*n.* 愉快，乐意，高兴，满意

to have/take the pleasure to do sth. (in/of doing sth.) 乐于做某事

(2)offer：*n. /v.* 报盘(包括商品、数量、价格、船期、支付方式、有效期等，通常与介词 for、of、on 连用)

常用搭配有：

to make an offer 报盘

to make sb. an offer for sth. 向某人报盘某商品

to offer sth. 报盘某商品

to offer sb. sth. 向某人报盘某商品

常用词组有：

to accept an offer 接受报盘　to decline an offer 拒绝报盘

to confirm an offer 确认报盘　to withdraw an offer 撤回报盘

to renew an offer 恢复报盘　to entertain an offer 考虑报盘

to extend an offer 延长报盘

(3)(be) subject to：以……为准，以……有效

e. g. ：we offer... subject to our final confirmation.

我方报盘……以我方最后确认有效。

6. article：*n.* 商品(单数)

7. Art. No. 商品号码，货号

8. standard export wooden case：标准出口木箱

9. payment：by confirmed, irrevocable L/C payable by draft at sight to be opened 30 days before the time of shipment.

付款：装船前 30 天开出保兑的、不可撤销的信用证见票即付.

10. We look forward to receiving your trial order. 我方期望能收到贵方试订单。

 **Letter 2   A non-firm offer**

July 10，2017

Dear Sirs，

Thank you for your enquiry of July 8 for our Groundnuts. In reply, we make you the following offer subject to our final confirmation：

Commodity：Shandong Groundnuts, Hand-picked.

Quantity：7,000 metric tons.

Price：RMB 2,000 net per metric ton CIF Hamburger.

Shipment：During September, 2011, from Qingdao.

Payment：by irrevocable L/C payable against draft at sight.

Insurance：ALL RISKS.

If you find the above acceptable, please fax us for our final confirmation.

Yours sincerely，

Lucia

Sales Manager

 **Notes**

1. a non-firm offer：（an offer without engagement）虚盘，一般没有有效期和约束力。以下是表示虚盘的用语：

（be）subject to our final confirmation 以我方最后确认为准

（be）subject to goods being unsold 以货物未售出为有效

（be）subject to prior sale 以先售为条件

（be）subject to change without notice 不经通知可以改变

（be）subject to market fluctuation 以市场波动为准

2. Groundnuts：落花生

3. In reply, we make you the following offer subject to our final confirmation. 兹回复，我方现给你方做出如下报盘，以我方最后确认为准。

4. hand-picked：用手挑选的，精选的

5. metric ton：公吨（重量单位）

6. Hamburger：汉堡（港口城市）

7. payment：by irrevocable L/C payable against draft at sight.

付款：即期不可撤销的信用证见票即付。

8. ALL RISKS：一切险

9. If you find the above acceptable, please fax us for our final confirmation. 如果贵方能接受上述报盘,请传真告知我方以便最终确认。

 **Letter 3   An offer on different quantities at certain discounts**

January 20, 2017

Dear Sirs,

We are in receipt of your enquiry of January 18 for 1,000 M/T walnut meat with many thanks. As per your enquiry, we are now offering as follows:

For 1,000 M/T of superior walnut meat, we offer RMB 5,000 per M/T FOB Tianjin or RMB 5,200 per M/T CIF Liverpool. Our goods will be packed in polyethylene woven bags, 10 kg and 15 kg each. We accept L/C payment. Shipment will be effected two weeks after the receipt of payment.

As our minimum order is 200 M/T to any European port, your order of 1,000 M/T will have our 3% discount. This preferential treatment is subject to your order before the end of November.

We hope the above information is of use to you and look forward to receiving your immediate reply.

Yours sincerely,

Susan

Sales Manager

Notes

1. We are in receipt of your enquiry of... for...: 我方收到贵方×月×日关于……的询盘。

2. As per your enquiry, we are now offering as follows: 根据贵方的询价,我方现报盘如下:

3. For 1,000 M/T of superior walnut meat, we offer RMB 5,000 per M/T FOB Tianjin or RMB 5,200 per M/T CIF Liverpool. 1,000 公吨优质核桃仁,我方的报价是天津离岸价每公吨 5000 元人民币,或利物浦到岸价每公吨 5200 元人民币。

(1)M/T: = metric ton,公吨

(2)superior:优良的、质量上乘的

superior goods 优等物品

superior quality 优质;等品,高级货品

superior performance 性能优越

be superior to 优于,比……好

e.g.: Our product is superior to all competitive products.

我方产品质量优于所有的竞争产品。

(3)offer:v. 报盘(某商品)

e.g.: We can offer you a quotation based on the international market.

我们可以按国际市场价格给贵方报价。

(4) FOB：= Free on Board，离岸价（价格术语）

CIF：= Cost, Insurance and Freight，到岸价（价格术语）

4. be packed in. . . ：用……包装

5. polyethylene woven bags：聚乙烯编织袋

6. Shipment will be effected two weeks after the receipt of payment. 装运会在收到货款后的两周内完成。

7. minimum order：= minimum order quantity（MOQ），最少订购量、起订量

8. This preferential treatment is subject to your order before the end of November. 此优惠以贵方 11 月底之前订购为有效。

9. We hope the above information is of use to you. 希望上述信息对贵方有用。

 Letter 4　Unable to make any offer because of out of stock

October 9，2017

Dear Sirs，

Fresh Ginger

In reply to your enquiry of October 7 for 30 metric tons of the captioned goods，we regret to advise that we are unable to make an offer for the time being owing to heavy demands. Furthermore，a fax to this effect has been sent to you today.

However，we shall not fail to inform you whenever a fresh supply is available.

Yours faithfully，

Lili

Sales Manager

 **Notes**

1. In reply to. . . ：兹回复、现回复

2. the captioned goods：标题项下的商品

e. g. ：We thank you for your Enquiry List No. 118 and enclose our Quotation No. 226 for the captioned goods.

感谢贵方第 118 号询价单，现随函附寄我方第 226 号标题项下的货物的报价。

3. We regret to advise that we are unable to make an offer for the time being owing to heavy demands. 我方抱歉告知，由于需求量过大，我们目前不能做出报价。

4. to this effect：提到该事；表示那个（或这个）意思，大意如此，表示类似的意思

5. We shall not fail to inform you whenever a fresh supply is available. 只要有新的供货，我们会通知贵方。

supply：n. 供应；供应量

e. g. ：Prices change according to supply and demand.

价格根据供应量和需求量而变化。

The market must be fed with an endless supply of goods.

　　必须源源不断地向市场提供商品。

常见的短语有：

supply and demand 供应与需求

the supply of...（某商品）的供应

in short supply 供不应求

supply chain 供应链；供给链；供需链

supply chain management 供应连锁管理

4.3　Writing Steps and Tips

Based on the above specimen letters, some essential writing steps and tips about business letters of quotations or offers can be clearly and accurately summed up into the following points:

Writing steps	Examples of expressions
(1)Stating thanks for one's enquiry and pleasure for making an offer 感谢对方的询盘,并乐意报盘	Thank you for your enquiry and for your interest in our products. Many thanks for your enquiry of... We thank for your enquiry and are pleased to make an offer as follows.
(2)Stating clearly all the terms about goods required 向对方提供所需商品的所有交易条件	We quote for this article at USD 10 per piece CIF Ningbo. We offer you 3,000 Bicycles at GBP 40. 00 per piece FOB London for delivery in November.
(3)Making clear the nature of the offer. For a firm offer, state the period of validity; for a non-firm offer, state the offer without engagement 明确报盘的类型。如果是实盘,明确有效期;如果是虚盘,表明报盘不具效力	This offer is to be withdrawn if not accepted by April 27. Price quoted is valid until September 18. This offer is subject to our final confirmation. This offer is subject to goods being unsold. This quotation is subject to the market fluctuation.
(4)Stating the hope for accepting the offer and receiving one's order 表达希望对方接受该报盘并早日订货的愿望	We look forward to your favorable reply at an earlier date. We hope that our offer will be satisfactory to you and anticipate your order earlier.

4.4　Useful Expressions on Quotations or Offers

　　1. Thank you for your enquiry of May 4 and we are pleased to send you our best quotation for Women's Shirts.

谢谢贵方 5 月 4 日的询盘,现向贵方报女衬衫的最低价。

2. We have learnt that there is a large demand for walnut meat in your market and take this opportunity of enclosing our quotation sheet No. 296 for your reference.

我方获悉贵地市场对核桃仁有较大需求,现寄上我方第 296 号报价单供参考。

3. We welcome your enquiry of December 6 and thank you for your interest in our products.

欢迎贵方 12 月 6 日的询盘,并感谢贵方对我方产品的兴趣。

4. In reply to your enquiry of July 16, we are sending you herewith our quotation together with various samples of leather boots closely resembling to what you want.

应贵方 7 月 16 日来函询问,现寄上我方的报价和几双式样不同的与贵方要求相近的皮靴样品。

5. We have much pleasure in enclosing a quotation sheet for our products and trust that their high quality will induce you to place a trial order.

我方非常高兴寄上产品报价单,我方相信我们的产品质量会促使贵方试订。

6. We quote for this article at USD 20 per case FOB Qingdao.

我方报此货 FOB 青岛价,每箱 20 美元。

7. We offer you 2,000 "Wuyang" Bicycles at GBP 30.00 per piece CIF London for delivery in December.

我方向贵方报盘 2000 辆五羊牌自行车,伦敦到岸价,每辆 30 英镑,12 月交货。

8. As requested, we are offering you the following subject to our final confirmation.

应要求,我方就如下货物向贵方报价,但以我方最后确认为准。

9. At your request, we now keep this firm offer open for a further 15 days from September 12.

按贵方要求,我方现将实盘有效期从 9 月 12 日起再延长 15 天。

10. We are making you a firm offer, subject to your reply reaching us before March 25.

现向贵方报实盘,以贵方 3 月 25 日复到为有效。

11. This offer is to be withdrawn if not accepted by April 17.

如果贵方没有在 4 月 17 前接受该报盘,它将无效。

12. This offer is subject to goods being unsold.

该报盘以货物未售出为有效。

13. We must stress that this offer is firm for three days only because of the heavy demand for the limited supplies of this line in stock.

我方必须强调,此报价仅有效 3 天,因为此类产品的存货有限而需求量过大。

14. We think you have made an excellent choice in selecting this line, and once you have seen the samples we are sure you will agree that this is unique both in design and color.

我方觉得贵方能选择此类产品完全是明智的。一旦贵方看到样品,我方确信贵方会认同此类产品的样式和颜色都是独一无二的。

15. Their excellent quality, attractive designs and reasonable prices at which we offer them will convince you that these materials are really of good value.

它们良好的品质、诱人的花样以及所报的合理价格将会使贵方相信这些料子是货真价实的。

16. As recently the goods required are in extremely short supply，we regret being unable to offer.

由于近来货源奇缺，歉难报盘。

17. We trust that you will be able to accept our offer，which shall be kept open against reply by fax.

我方确信贵方会接受我方的报盘。此报盘至复传真为止有效。

18. As the prices quoted are exceptionally low and likely to rise，we would advise you to accept the offer without delay.

由于所报价格特别低，并可能上涨，我方建议贵方立即接受此报盘。

19. As we have been receiving a rush of orders now，we would advise you to place your order as soon as possible.

由于我方目前正收到大量订单，因此我方建议贵方立即订购。

20. As it is the first transaction between us，we are making you a special offer.

因为这是我们的第一笔生意，所以特报此优惠发盘。

4.5　Exercises

Ⅰ. Multiple choices.

1. Thank you for your letter of May 9，_____ which you offered us 12,500 yards of printed shirting on the following terms and conditions.

    A. of   B. in   C. to   D. with

2. Please let us _____ your firm offer before the end of this month.

    A. having   B. to have   C. had   D. have

3. A firm offer _____ a time limit for acceptance.

    A. must specify   B. may specify

    C. sometimes specify   D. may specify

4. We are offering you goods _____ the high quality.

    A. at   B. for   C. of   D. with

5. This price will remain _____ for ten days from the date of the letter.

    A. invaluable   B. good   C. valid   D. valuable

6. We would recommend you _____ this offer.

    A. to accept   B. accepting   C. accepted   D. accept

7. If you are interested，we will send you a sample lot _____ charge.

    A. for   B. free of   C. with   D. within

8. For your information，our products enjoy a ready _____ in Europe.

    A. sale   B. selling   C. sail   D. sell

9. We place this order with you _____ the understanding that the discount is 10%.

A. through　　　　B. with　　　　　C. based on　　　　D. on

10. _____ a limited supply is available at present，we would ask you to act quickly.

　　A. Because　　　B. Since　　　　　C. As　　　　　　D. On account of

Ⅱ. Translate the following terms and expressions.

1. a firm offer

2. make sb. an offer for sth.

3. without engagement

4. subject to

5. as requested

6. 虚盘

7. 报价单

8. 市场价格

9. 报盘有效期

10. 以我方最后确认为准

Ⅲ. Translate the following sentences into English.

1. 我方对贵公司在 7 月 18 日的询盘表示感谢。按照贵方要求，我方愿意对产品报如下实盘。

2. 现按你方要求报盘如下，以我方最后确认为准。

3. 现报盘如下，以我方时间 10 月 15 日下午 5 时前复到有效。

4. 如果贵方能订购 600 打或者 600 打以上，我方将提供 8% 的折扣。

5. 我方相信贵方会满意我们的报价，盼订货。

6. 我们的产品物美价廉。

Ⅳ. Translate the following sentences into Chinese.

1. Referring to your letter of August 9 in which you enquired for plastic toys, we are pleased to fax you an offer as follows.

2. We are sending you a firm offer, subject to your reply here before 4 p. m. our time, June 12.

3. This offer must be withdrawn if not accepted within ten days.

4. We are sure that these goods will meet your requirements, and we look forward to your first order.

5. We offer you such low price totally because we hope it will be a good start of our long business relation.

6. We believe that you will place a large order with us owing to the high quality and reasonable price of our products.

Ⅴ. Writing practice.

Draft a letter of offer according to the following points：

1. 感谢贵公司 9 月 18 日的询盘。得知我方产品"工艺包(handicraft bags)"在贵方市场需求量很大，不胜欣慰。

2. 兹复贵公司 9 月 18 日询价函，报价如下：

(1)工艺包每个 9.00 美元(纽约到岸价 CIF NEW YORK)。

(2)包装:纸箱(Carton),每箱 25 个。

(3)超过 2000 个的订货给予 5% 的折扣。

3.我们将迅速办理贵公司的订货事宜。

Chapter 5　Counter-offers and Acceptance

Learning objectives

To know about the meaning of counter-offers and acceptance.

To master writing letters of making counter-offers.

To master the words and expressions related to letters of making counter-offers.

5.1　Brief Introduction

In business negotiation, the buyer should give a response to the seller's offer after receiving it. If the buyer (or the offeree) and the seller (or the offeror) agree on all terms and conditions of an offer, both parties can make a contract and conclude business. This refers to the acceptance of the offer. Acceptance is a final and unconditional expression of assent to the terms of an offer and willingness to make a deal and sign a contract. Since an acceptance is an unconditional agreement with the terms proposed by an offeror, the terms of an acceptance must be in accordance with the terms of an offer.

On the contrary, if the buyer finds any terms or conditions unacceptable in the offer, he can negotiate with the seller and make a counter-offer to show his disagreement and state his own terms instead. Making a counter-offer automatically rejects the prior offer, and requires an acceptance under the terms of the counter-offer.

When the seller receives the buyer's counter-offer, and finds some terms and conditions unacceptable to him, he will also state his own opinions in a letter, which is called as a counter-counter-offer. This process can go on for several rounds till business is finalized or called off.

To sum up, a counter-offer is virtually a partial rejection of the original offer and a counter proposal initiated by the buyer or the offeree. It is a new offer, indicating that business will be negotiated on the renewed basis.

In writing a letter of making a counter-offer, the writer should explain reasons for rejection and put forward his proper and reasonable counter-offer suggestions in a courtesy way. Writing the letter of counter-offer always based on the following principles:

(1)Be courteous but directly tell the subject;

(2)List what you disagree;

(3)Clearly make your suggestions.

5.2 Specimen Letters

 Letter 1 Buyer's counter-offer for a high price

> December 8，2017
>
> Dear Sirs，
>
> Thank you for your offer of December 4 for 10,000 sets of Panasonic 2066 Color TV at USD 500 per set CIF Hamburger.
>
> In reply，we regret to inform you that your price is too high. Market information tells us that other brands in the same quality have been sold here at a level about 20% lower than yours.
>
> Although we appreciate the high quality of your Color TV, the difference in price is still a wide gap. To step up the business, we make a counter-offer as follows：12,000 Panasonic 2066 Color TV, at USD 350 per set CIF Hamburger.
>
> We trust that you will find our counter-offer reasonable and we are awaiting your prompt reply.
>
> Yours faithfully，
>
> (Signature)

 **Notes**

1. Thank you for your offer of... for... at...：感谢贵方×月×日以……价格报价……

2. Hamburger：汉堡（德国港口城市）

3. We regret to inform you that your price is too high. 我方抱歉告知,贵方的价格太高。

4. Market information tells us that...：我方根据市场信息获悉……

5. The difference in price is still a wide gap. 这种价格上的差异仍然存在较大的差距。

6. To step up the business，we make a counter-offer as follows：为了促进交易,我方做出如下还盘：

counter-offer：n./v. 还盘,还价

make a counter-offer 还盘,做出还价

e.g.：Our counter-offer is well in line with the international market fair and reasonable.
  我们的还盘完全符合国际市场的价格水平,公平,合理。

  As there is really demand for the captioned goods in Italy，we are now counter-offering as follows.
  因为意大利确实对标题货物需求量很大,我方现还盘如下。

7. We trust that you will find our counter-offer reasonable. 我方相信贵方会觉得我们的还盘是合理的。

find sth. reasonable/acceptable 认为合理/可以接受

find the price favorable 认为价格优惠

Letter 2   Buyer's counter-offer for commission and payment terms

Dear Sirs,

　　Your offer of September 18 for groundnuts and the samples have been received, for which we thank you.

　　We would request you to give us an 8% commission instead of 3% and to accept payment by D/P at sight because of the cost of using L/C, as we are working with other suppliers on these terms.

　　We trust you will be glad to confirm the above terms by e-mail at an early date, so that we may send in our formal order with detailed shipping instructions accordingly.

Yours sincerely,

Susan

 **Notes**

　　1. Your offer of... for... have been received, for which we thank you. 贵方×月×日对……的报价已收到,非常感谢。

　　2. We would request you to give us...：请提供我方……

　　3. to accept payment by D/P at sight：接受即期付款交单的付款方式

　　D/P：Documents against Payment 付款交单

　　4. L/C：Letter of Credit 信用证

　　5. supplier：供应商

　　6. to confirm the above terms by e-mail at an early date：尽早电邮确认上述交易条件

　　7. We may send in our formal order with detailed shipping instructions accordingly. 我方可以据此递交正式合同和详细的装运须知。

　　(1)send in：=deliver,递交,呈上

　　(2)shipping instructions：装运须知

 Letter 3   Seller's counter-counter-offer for price reduction

Dear Sirs,

　　We learn from your letter of May 10th that our price for women's suits is found to be too high to conclude business.

　　We regret to inform you that your counter-offer is not in keeping with the current market. Our price has been accepted by other buyers in your city, at which considerable transactions have been done, and that enquiries have kept flooding in over the past few months. It is in view of our long-standing business relations that we consider making you a firm offer at such a favorable price.

　　We hope you will reconsider it and fax us your order for our confirmation at your earliest convenience.

Yours sincerely,

Jackie

 **Notes**

1. Our price for women's suits is found to be too high to conclude business. 我方女士套装的价格太高而无法成交。

too high to conclude business 太高而无法成交

conclude business/come to business/strike a bargain 成交,缔结交易

2. We regret to inform you that your counter-offer is not in keeping with the current market. 我方抱歉告知贵方,贵方的还盘与现行市场不符。

3. considerable transactions:大笔交易

4. enquiries have kept flooding:询价源源不断

5. It is in view of our long-standing business relations that we consider making you a firm offer at such a favorable price. 正是因为我们长期的业务关系,我方才考虑以优惠价格报实盘。

make a firm offer at a favorable price 以优惠价格报实盘

6. We hope you will reconsider it and fax us your order for our confirmation at your earliest convenience. 我方希望贵方能重新考虑,并在方便之时传真贵方订单,供我方确认。

 Letter 4 Seller's acceptance of the counter-offer for price reduction

Dear Sirs,

We have received your letter of December 15.

It is regretful for us to see that you cut down the price of our Diamond Brand electric fans too sharp, but considering our long term of business relationship, we decide to accept your counter-offer on condition that cash must be paid within three months of the delivery date.

We await your order at an earliest date.

Yours sincerely,

Jackie

 **Notes**

1. It is regretful for us to see that...:我方抱歉地表示……

2. cut down the price:降价,削价

3. We decide to accept your counter-offer on condition that cash must be paid within three months of the delivery date. 我方决定接受贵方还盘,条件是要在交货期的三个月内用现金付款。

accept your counter-offer 接受贵方还盘

on condition that... 条件是……;假如,如果

delivery date 交货期

4. We await your order at an earliest date. 盼贵方早日订购。

5.3   Writing Steps and Tips

Based on the above specimen letters, some essential writing steps and tips about business letters of counter-offers can be clearly and accurately summed up into the following points.

Writing steps	Examples of expressions
(1) Expressing thanks for the offer or quotation 对发盘人的报价或发盘表示感谢	Thank you for your prompt reply and detailed offer.
(2) Expressing regret at inability to accept and explaining 表示无法接受发盘并说明原因	The price you offer is out of line with the market, so it is beyond what is acceptable to us.
(3) Making a counter-offer and stating suggestions 对所希望的交易条件提出还盘建议	In view of our long-standing business relationship, we make you the following counter-offer. To step up trade, we counter-offer as follows...
(4) Expressing the hope 希望对方能接受所提出的还盘建议	We hope that you will consider our counter-offer favorably and reply as soon as possible.

5.4   Useful Expressions on Counter-offers and Acceptance

1. Your price is on the high side and we have to counter-offer as follows, subject to your reply received by us on or before November 8.

贵方价格偏高,我方不得不作如下还盘,以我方在 11 月 8 日或以前收到贵方答复为有效。

2. Our counter-offer is well founded.

我方的还盘还是很合理的。

3. We make a counter-offer to you of USD 200 per metric ton CIF Seattle.

我方还价为每公吨西雅图到岸价 200 美元。

4. We can't accept your offer unless the price is reduced by 5%.

除非贵方愿意减价 5%,否则我们无法接受报盘。

5. Your competitors are offering considerably lower prices and unless you can reduce your quotations, we shall have to buy elsewhere.

贵方竞争对手的报价要低很多。除非贵方降价,否则我方得从他处购买。

6. You could benefit from higher sale with a little concession, say a 3% reduction.

只要稍作让步,比方说降价 2%,就可得到一大笔交易。

7. This is our rock-bottom price, we can't make any further reduction.

这是我方的最低价格了,我们不能再让了。

8. Our price has been reduced to the minimum.

我方价格已经降到最低限度。

9. The best we can do is to make a reduction of 5% in our previous quotation.

在前一次的报价中减让 5% 是我方所能做出的最大让步。

10. Considering our long-standing friendly business relation, we can allow you reduction of 5% in our price.

考虑到我们双方长期友好的贸易关系,我方同意在原价基础上让利 5%。

11. Much to our regret, we cannot entertain business at your price, since it is out of line with the prevailing market, being 10% lower than the average.

很遗憾我方不能考虑按贵方价格成交,因为贵方价格与现时市场不一致,要比一般价格低 10%。

12. To develop our market in your place, we have decided to accept your counter-offer as an exceptional case.

为了在贵地拓展我公司的市场,我方决定破例接受贵方的还盘。

13. We regret to note that you have turned down our counter-offer.

很遗憾得知贵方已拒绝我方的还盘。

14. It is hoped that you would seriously take it into consideration and let us have your reply very soon.

希望你方能认真考虑我方的建议并尽快回复。

5.5 Exercises

Ⅰ. Multiple choices.

1. _____ you make a reduction of 5%, we will have to decline your offer this time.

    A. Except   B. Unless   C. When   D. As

2. We wish to direct your attention to the excellent quality of our products _____ price.

    A. been passed through   B. passed on

    C. subject to   D. instead of

3. If you can _____ us a 4% discount, we shall give you our initial order amounting to GBP 25,000.

    A. allow   B. guarantee   C. pay   D. cost

4. If you accept our counter-offer, we shall _____ our end-users to buy from you.

    A. allow   B. demand   C. advise   D. offer

5. We _____ your counter-offer but find it too low to accept.

    A. appreciate   B. grateful   C. accept   D. refuse

6. Since your price is _____ with the prevailing market, it is not impossible for the buyers at our end to accept.

    A. out of line   B. in line   C. beyond scope   D. following

7. A comparison of your offer _____ our regular suppliers shows that their figures

are more favorable.

　　A. with what of　　B. with which of　　C. with whom of　　D. with that of

8. We place this order _____ condition that the discount is 15%.

　　A. if　　　　　　　B. on　　　　　　　C. suppose　　　　　D. should

9. We don't think we can put the business through _____ you revise your terms and conditions.

　　A. only if　　　　B. in addition　　　C. expect　　　　　D. unless

10. _____ our long-term business relations and our amicable cooperation prospects，we suggest that you accept our terms.

　　A. For which　　B. Because of　　　C. In iew of　　　　D. In that

Ⅱ. Translate the following sentences into English.

1. 鉴于我们之间长期的业务关系,特做此还盘。

2. 我们认为你方价格不合适,我们各让一半好吗?

3. 由于原料价格不断上涨,歉难满足你方再次降价的要求。

4. 接受你们现实的报价意味着我们将有巨大亏损,更不用谈利润了。

5. 我们不能考虑按你方价格成交,因为你方价格与市价不符。

6. 通过贵方全力合作,我方能够以你修订的价格试订一批货。

Ⅲ. Translate the following sentences into Chinese.

1. We regret to inform you that the price you quoted is on the high side though we appreciate the good quality of your products.

2. As business has been done extensively in your market at this price，we regret that we cannot accept your counter-offer.

3. We agree to your price but should like to know if you are prepared to grant us a discount of 5% for a quantity of 2,000.

4. The price you counter-offered is out of line with the market，so it is beyond what is acceptable to us.

5. We regret that it is impossible to accept your counter-offer，even to meet you half way，because the price of raw material has advanced by 20%.

Ⅳ. Writing practice.

Draft a letter according to the following points.

某海外公司客户 Paul 收到某外贸公司业务员 Steven 的发盘函后,要对其进行回复。请以 Paul 的名义写一封针对 Steven 发盘的回函,具体要求如下:

1. 表示收到对方的发盘函,并表示感谢。

2. 很遗憾告知对方,你地客户认为他们产品的价格偏高。

3. 提出还盘建议:单价变为每件 16.50 英镑,CIFC 2% 利物浦。

4. 希望对方做出尽快回复。

Chapter 6   Orders and Their Fulfillment

Learning objectives

To know about the meaning of an order and its fulfillment.

To master writing letters of orders and their fulfillment.

To master the useful expressions about letters of orders and their fulfillment.

6.1   Brief Introduction

An order is a request to supply a specified quantity of goods. It is given by the buyer. An order may be given by letter, faxes, e-mails or orally at a meeting. Usually, business uses an order form to obtain goods from suppliers. When a form is not available, a letter is needed for the order. When writing an order letter, you must include all the essential qualities so that your order is clear and complete. You should use the listing format of the order form as a guide to giving information about the following matters:

1. An accurate and full description of goods required;

2. Catalogue numbers, quantities, prices, and terms of payment agreed upon;

3. Delivery requirements (place, date, packing, shipping marks, mode of transportation, etc.).

When a seller receives the "first" order from a new customer, he must write a letter to acknowledge the order. The letter should be:

1. Express pleasure at receiving the order;

2. Add a favorable comment on the goods ordered;

3. Include an assurance of prompt and careful attention;

4. Draw attention to other products likely to be interested;

5. Hope for further orders.

However, there are times when sellers cannot accept buyers' orders because the goods required are out of stock or prices and specifications have been changed. In such circumstances, it is advisable to recommend suitable substitutes, make counter-offers and persuade buyers to accept them.

6.2 Specimen Letters

Letter 1   A trial order

Dear Sirs,

We are happy to enclose our trial order No. SidB-8822, for 325 Burda Ladies' Car Coats, size medium, navy blue color; at $ 98.65 per coat, subject to six percent quantity discount. Please sign the duplicate of the enclosed order form and return it to us as your acknowledgment.

As stated in your quotation of April 8, we may expect immediate shipment from stock. We are looking forward to your acknowledgment.

Yours faithfully,

(Signature)

Notes

1. We are happy to enclose our trial order...:很荣幸为您随函附上试用订单号为……
类似的表达方式如下：

a)Please find enclosed our order...

b)Enclosed you will find our order...

c)We are pleased to enclose our order...

2. at...per...:单价为……

3. subject to...:以……（6%的折扣率）;受制于;使服从;受……管制

e.g.：These prices are subject to variation.

这些价格可能变更。

4. Please sign the duplicate of the enclosed order form and return it to us as your acknowledgment. 请确认后签订随函订单副本并寄还我方。

5. As stated in your quotation of...:正如贵方在……报价中的要求

6. ...expect immediate shipment from stock:我方希望尽快转船运货

Letter 2   Enclosing an order

Dear Sirs,

We thank you for your quotation of July 3 for the supply of vacuum bottles and find your terms acceptable. We are pleased to enclose our order, No. 993 for 1,500 unbreakable stainless-steel vacuum bottles (Cat. No. 330C 1-quart Bottle) at $ 19.65 per bottle.

We would appreciate delivery within one month and look forward to your acknowledgment.

Yours sincerely,

Susan

 **Notes**

1. We thank you for your quotation of... :感谢贵方在……的报价

2. find your terms acceptable:接受贵方条件

3. We are pleased to enclose our order. 很高兴订购随函附上订单。

4. at... per... :单价为……

5. We would appreciate delivery within one month. 我方希望在一个月内交货。

 Letter 3 A favorable reply to an order

Dear Sirs，

Thank you for your order (SB-8802) for three general lightweight hand trucks. We are currently processing this order，which we expect to have ready for shipment by Ameri-Express Services within two weeks. Our shipping department will notify you in advance.

Thank you for doing business with us.

Yours faithfully，

(Signature)

 **Notes**

1. Thank you for your order for... :非常感谢您对……的订购

2. We are currently processing this order:我方正在备货

3. We expect to have ready for shipment:预计……发货

 Letter 4 An unfavorable reply to an order

Dear Sirs，

Thank you for your order No. C876-DD for 125 Do-It-Yourself Paint Machines. However，we are unable at this time to fulfill this order due to a fire in our manufacturing plant in New Orleans three days ago. We intend to resume production next week and expect to deliver your order early next month.

We apologize for the delay and hope it will not cause you serious inconvenience.

Yours sincerely，

Susan

 **Notes**

1. We are unable at this time to fulfill this order. 我方目前不能履行此订单。

类似的表达方式如下：

a)We regret that we cannot accept your order.

b)We are unable to accept your order at the price you requested of...

2. due to:由于

3. intend to:打算

4. resume production:恢复生产

resume ＜n.＞简历；摘要；＜v.＞重新开始，恢复

6.3　Writing Steps and Tips

Based on the above specimen letters, some essential writing steps and tips about business letters for orders and their fulfillment can be clearly and accurately summed up into the following points.

1. An Order Letter(订货信函)

Writing steps	Examples of expressions
(1) Showing thanks for one's letter and stating placing an order with sb. 感谢对方来函，决定订购货物	We are in receipt of your letter of... and are pleased to place an order with you for the following goods.
(2)Confirming the transaction terms as agreed on 确认所订购货物的交易条件，如商品详情、价格、付款方式、包装、装运等	(1) Enclosed please find our Order No. B5421 for... (2) We would like to confirm that payment is to be made by irrevocable letter of credit 注：为使内容清晰，这部分可以列表说明
(3)Expressing the hope 表示希望对方及时处理订单以及将来继续订购的可能性	We will submit further orders, if this one is completed to our satisfaction.

2. A Letter to Acknowledge and Accept an Order (确认并接受订货信)

Writing steps	Examples of expressions
(1)Showing pleasure and thanks for receiving the order 感谢对方订购货物	Thank you for your order No. 354GF.
(2)be able to deliver the goods and confirm the transaction terms 表示能够供货，并确认交易条件或附寄合同	(1) We have these clocks in stock and will be able to deliver them before March 6th you requested. (2) We enclose our S/C No. 20 in duplicate. Please sign and return one copy for our file.
(3)add a favorable comment on the goods ordered 称赞所订之货，或者提醒对方注意事项	We are sure you will be pleased with this new line of wrist watches.
(4)hope for further orders 告知对方会及时认真履行订单，并希望再次收到对方更多的订单	We are looking forward to pleasant business relations with your company.

3. A Letter to Decline an Order（婉拒订货信）

Writing steps	Examples of expressions
(1)Showing pleasure and thanks for receiving the order 感谢对方订购货物	(1) Thank you for your order No. 118 of… (2) We are pleased to receive your order of…
(2)Showing the regret for being unable to accept the order and explaining 对婉拒订货表示歉意并做出合理的解释	(1)It is much regretful that we have to decline your order because there is no stock of the goods ordered currently. (2)We are very sorry to decline your order because…
(3) Recommending another substitute supplied from stock, if possible 若有可提供的替代货品,建议对方使用替代品	(1)We would like to recommend an excellent substitute, which is superior to the article required in quality, but the price is almost the same. (2) At present we can supply… from stock, and they are of the same quality and also fashionable.
(4)Hoping for one's favorable reply 希望收到对方回复	(1)We hope to receive your order again. (2) We anticipate your good news next time.

6.4　Useful Expressions on Orders and Their Fulfillment

1. Please find enclosed our official order form No. 338A for fifty（50）Model B Regina compact disc players.

随函附上正式订单,订单号为 No. 338A,订购 50 个 B 型号 ReginaCD 唱机。

2. This fax will confirm our order—placed by telephone this morning with your representative, Janet Gaynor—for 100 Annis pocket thermometers Model F4.

谨以本传真确认今天早上与你方代表 JanetGaynor 的电话,电话订购 100 台 F4 型 Annis 迷你温度计的订单。

3. We hereby confirm our telephone order for 25 sets of your special Quartz Clock (see page six of your summer catalog) at $89.50 per clock, minus two percent cash discount.

我们确认电话订购的 25 台特制石英表(请看第六页目录),单价 89.5 美元,并有 2% 现金支付折扣。

4. We would like to emphasize that this is a trial order. If the quality of your merchandise is up to sample, we expect to place substantial orders at regular intervals.

请注意此次为试订单。如贵方提供货物质量与样本一致,我方会定期大量订购。

5. As agreed in our telephone conversation of August 12, we will pay half the amount your invoice when the goods are delivered at our warehouse in Fayetteville, Maryland, and

the remainder within 30 days, deducting three percent discount.

按照 8 月 12 日电话会议中的约定,待贵方货物抵达我方位于马里兰州 Fayetvill 的仓库,我方将支付发票金额的一半货款,余款在 30 日之内交付并且有 3% 的折扣。

6. We place this trial order on the clear understanding that delivery to our warehouse in San Diego, Califormia, has to take place before May 1. Therefore, we reserve the right to cancel this order and refuse delivery after this date.

我方必须澄清,此次试订单务必在 5 月 1 日之前运达我方位于加州圣地亚哥的仓库中,如逾期抵达,我方有保留取消此次订单的权利。

7. You will find detailed instructions regarding marking and packing on the attached sheet.

在附件中,您会发现关于商标和包装问题的详细说明。

8. When packing, please wrap each part separately in soft material.

装运时,请用柔软材料分别包装每一部分。

9. Please, limit the overall length of any one crate to two yards.

请把每个装货箱总长度限制在 2 码。

10. Your order No. 8502 for 100 anti-theft auto locks is being processed and will be ready for shipment on October 13.

贵方订购的 100 把防盗自动锁,订单编号 NO. 8502 正在备货,并将于 10 月 13 日装船。

11. Thank you for your order No. 00833, which has been completed and transported to the Port of Newark, New Jersey, where it will be loaded onto the Denver. The freighter sails for Hamburg on April 11 and arrives on April 20.

感谢您的订单,编号 No. 00833,现已完成并运至新泽西的组瓦克港口准备装载到凡佛市,货船将于 4 月 11 日出发,4 月 20 日抵达汉堡。

12. We are pleased to inform you that your order (GWRK/229) is being processed and will be dispatched by airfreight to Naples on July 2.

很高兴通知贵方,您的订单(GWRK/229)正在准备中,并将于 7 月 2 日空运至那不勒斯。

13. Your order (No. 88QE) will be dispatched immediately upon receipt of your remittance of DM 5, 700. 69 as per the attached pro-forma invoice.

一收到按照随函所附形式发票金额的你方汇款 5700.69DM,我方将尽快安排发货(订单编号 88QE)。

14. We enclose our pro-forma invoice for $ 21,875.40. Please inform us what arrangements you have made for payment. On receipt of your remittance we will forward your order immediately FOB Sumter, Mississippi.

附件是形式发票,金额为 21,875.40 美元。请告知贵方的付款方式。一收到汇款,我方将尽快以密西西比州萨姆特市的离岸价发货。

15. We enclose our pro-forma invoice. Your order will be ready for immediate shipment to Canmore, North Dakota, when we receive your remittance.

附件是形式发票。一收到贵方汇款,我方将货物立即装船运至北达科他州的坎莫尔。

16. We are unable to give you a firm date for delivery until the necessary documents are

received.

我们不能给出确切的交货时间,直到收到所需的单据为止。

17. We are sorry that we cannot supply your order on the credit terms you requested in your fax of March 3.

很遗憾,我们不能按照贵方 3 月 3 日传真中的付款条件提供货物。

18. We have been very pleased to serve you and hope to establish a pleasant business connection with your company.

我们很高兴能为您服务,希望与贵公司建立良好的商务往来。

19. We hope that this initial order will lead to further business.

我们希望此首次订购会带来进一步的合作。

20. We appreciate your business and look forward to serving you again soon.

我们感谢您的订购并希望尽快再次为您服务。

6.5　Exercises

Ⅰ. Multiple choices.

1. _____ please find a price list of our new products.

    A. Enclosing　　　B. Enclose　　　　C. Enclosed　　　　D. Enclosure

2. Could you make us a firm _____ Shoes.

    A. of　　　　　　B. for　　　　　　C. off　　　　　　D. at

3. We are a state corporation, specializing _____ the export of oilseeds.

    A. in　　　　　　B. at　　　　　　C. on　　　　　　D. with

4. In the meantime, please _____ us informed _____ developments _____ your ends.

    A. keep, with, at　B. have, by, in　　C. touch, with, on　D. fail, by, to

5. We expect to put _____ the deal.

    A. through　　　　B. with　　　　　C. on　　　　　　D. up with

6. If the price is _____ us, we would sign a long-term contract with you.

    A. acceptable to　B. received by　　C. reached to　　D. accept by you

7. We _____ this _____ a good start for our long-term friendship.

    A. wish, is　　　　B. hope, was　　C. wish, must　　D. hope, will be

8. If your _____ prices are offered, we are interested _____ a large order for your electric cookers.

    A. are reasonable, place　　　　　B. competitive, in placing

    C. workable, to book　　　　　　D. are best, in book

9. We would like to have _____ information about your business application software advertised _____ the September 26's newspaper business week.

    A. farthest, of　　B. furthest, in　　C. farther, about　D. furthest, on

10. Thank you for your letter of September 21 asking us to _____ you 1,000 "MD"

brand electric cooker for shipment March.

      A. offer   B. make   C. give   D. send

Ⅱ. Translate the following terms and expressions.

1. be much obliged if you...

2. be prepared to...

3. regarding (concerning)...

4. would be appreciated

5. as for (＝as to)

6. 修正办货单

7. 保兑行

8. 撤销订单

9. 试销货物

10. 商业证明书

Ⅲ. Translate the following sentences into English.

1. 你们也许知道,我市场急需该货。我们认为有必要强调必须按时装运。你方任何延迟装运将有损我们今后的业务。

2. 附上300辆自行车的试购订单一纸。如货物质量能使我方满意,今后我们将大量订购。

3. 我们对在沪举行的谈判结果感到满意。随函附上我97号订单一纸,订购500只闹钟,以便在我市场试销。我们相信你们会十分仔细地履行这一订单。

4. 你公司8月10日来函收悉,内附有关第100号订单订购500台缝纫机的销售确认书第90SP—5861号一式两份。今签退一份请查收。

5. 关于我方向你公司订购的500台缝纫机,我们已收到你方销售合同4845号。

6. 我们正殷切地等候你方的信用证,收到后我们立即安排装运。

7. 兹随函退回销售合同一份,我方已会签该合同。

8. 此试销订单,请先发来35台,以便开发市场。如成功,随后必有较大数量的定单。

9. 请每批另寄发票一份。

10. 可以肯定,我们会非常认真地履行你方订单,以致完全满意。

Ⅳ. Translate the following sentences into Chinese.

1. We may place considerable orders with you if your quality is satisfactory.

2. Enclosed is our order for 300 sets of Transistor Radios T432.

3. Your terms are satisfactory and we enclose an order.

4. We believe that the high quality of our products will induce you to place a trial order with us.

5. Thank you very much for your letter of June 5 with patterns and price list. We have made our choice and take pleasure in enclosing our Indent No. 342.

6. We enclose our revised order sheet No. 888 for 150,000 yards of printed cotton. We are looking forward to your confirmation of this order and also the sales note.

7. With reference to your letter of May 6, we are pleased to give an order for the follow-

ing.

8. Thank you for your offer of June 5. Your prices and quality are satisfactory and we are sending you an order as follows.

9. Please supply 5,000 tons of coal in accordance with the details in our order No. 114.

10. This is a trial order. Please send us 35 sets only so that we may tap the market. If successful, we will give you larger orders in the future.

Ⅴ. Writing practice.

Draft a letter according to the following points:

Reply from the manager of Sky Industrial Promotion Co., Ltd

Date: Aug. 20, 2017

Dear Sir or Madam:

Your offer of Aug. 19 has been accepted and we are glad to place our order NO. SIP0819 as follows:

ART. NO. 1001USD0. 76/PC FOB XIAMEN

ART. NO. 1003 USD0. 81/PC FOB XIAMEN

ART. NO. 1005 USD0. 85/PC FOB XIAMEN

Other terms and conditions are the same as we agreed before.

As this is the very first transaction we have concluded, your cooperation would be very much appreciated. Please send us your sales confirmation in duplicate for counter-signature.

Yours faithfully

Sky Industrial Promotion Co., Ltd.

Kevin Cluze (manager)

操作要求:

请制作售货确认书,要求条款内容全面、具体。

销售确认书

SALES CONTRACT

卖方 SELLER：		编号 NO. ：	
		日期 DATE：	
		地点 SIGNED IN：	
买方 BUYER：			

买卖双方同意以下条款达成交易：

This contract is made by and agreed between the BUYER and SELLER ，in accordance with the terms and conditions stipulated below.

1. 商品号 Art No.	2. 品名及规格 Commodity & Specification	3. 数量 Quantity	4. 单价及价格条款 Unit Price & Trade Terms	5. 金额 Amount
允许 With	溢短装，由卖方决定 More or less of shipment allowed at the sellers' option			

6. 总值 Total Value	
7. 包装 Packing	
8. 唛头 Shipping Marks	
9. 装运期及运输方式 Time of Shipment & means of Transportation	
10. 装运港及目的地 Port of Loading & Destination	
11. 保险 Insurance	
12. 付款方式 Terms of Payment	
13. 备注 Remarks	

The Buyer	The Seller

Chapter 7　Terms of Payment

Learning objectives

　　To know about the major terms of payment and payment instruments.

　　To be familiar with the definition and parties of L/C, and the procedure of using documentary L/C.

　　To master how to write letters of urging to establish, amending L/C and useful expressions.

　　To master useful expressions about terms of payment.

7.1　Brief Introduction

Payment is important and complicated in international business. It refers to the settlements of debts or the transfer of currency.

International payment mainly involves in payment terms, payment instruments and payment time and place.

Terms of payment in international settlement refers to the way used to settle debt and liability between individuals, enterprises and groups in different countries. It defines the conditions under which the seller and buyer agree to settle the financial amount of the Sales Contract. There are three major terms of payment in international settlement: the letter of credit, remittance and collection.

Remittance refers to the importer remits money to the exporter on his initiative through a bank according to the terms and time stipulated in the contract. So the parties in remittance generally involve in the remitter, the payee, the remitting bank and the paying bank. There are three types of remittance: mail transfer (M/T), telegraphic transfer (T/T) and demand draft (D/D). Whatever types of remittance, the document is always sent to the importer directly by the exporter and the bank does not involve in. So remittance is mostly used in payment in advance, commission payment, sample fee payment, cash with order, cash on delivery and open account trade.

Collection means the handling by banks of financial documents or commercial documents in accordance with instructions received, so as to obtain payment or acceptance, or deliver documents against payment or against acceptance, or deliver documents on other terms and conditions. So the parties in collection refer to principal, remitting bank, collecting bank, presenting bank and drawee. There are two types of collection: clean collection and documentary collection. Clean collection means collection of financial documents not accompanied by commercial documents. Documentary collection can be divided into documents against payment (D/P) and documents against acceptance (D/A).

The letter of credit (L/C) is a written undertaking by the issuing bank to the beneficiary, under which the bank undertakes to pay the beneficiary a sum certain in money within a designated time period and against any stipulated terms and documents. L/C is a reliable method of payment, facilitating trade with unknown buyers and giving protection to both sellers and buyers. The parties in L/C mainly include applicant, the issuing bank, the advising bank, beneficiary, the negotiating bank and the paying bank.

Sometimes the buyer fails to establish the L/C, or the L/C doesn't reach the seller in time, but goods ordered are ready or delivery date is approaching, then a letter has to be sent to the buyer to urge him to expedite the L/C or to ascertain its whereabouts. Messages urging establishment of L/C must be written with tact, because their aim is to persuade the buyer to cooperate more closely and in fact to fulfill his obligations, otherwise they will give offence to the buyer and bring about unhappy consequences. So you should take a polite note to say your request or purpose.

After receiving the relevant L/C, the seller (beneficiary) should first of all make a thorough examination to see whether the clauses in the L/C conform to the terms stated in the Sales Contract. If any differences or discrepancies are found in the L/C, the seller should send an advice to the buyer, asking him to make amendment. That is the L/C amendment.

7.2   Specimen Letters

 Letter 1   Urging establishment of L/C

Dear Sirs,

The goods under the S/C No. PL664 have already been ready for shipment. In addition, the date of delivery is approaching, but we still have not received your covering L/C to date.

Please do your utmost to expedite the L/C so as to enable us to effect shipment within the stipulated time. In order to avoid subsequent amendments, please see to it that the L/C stipulations conform to the terms of the contract.

We are looking forward to receiving your L/C soon.

Yours sincerely,

Betty

 **Notes**

1. (be) ready for shipment: 备妥待运
2. The date of delivery is approaching. 交货期临近。

3. We still have not received your covering L/C to date. 我方至今未收到贵方相关信用证。

4. Please do your utmost to expedite the L/C. 请尽力加速开证。

expedite：*v.* ＝ hurry up，催促、加速完成

5. effect shipment：安排装运

6. within the stipulated time：在规定的时间内

stipulated：规定的

stipulate：*v.* 规定

stipulation：*n.* 规定，条款

7. subsequent amendments：往后的修改

8. Please see to it that the L/C stipulations conform to the terms of the contract. 请务必使信用证条款与合同条款完全一致。

conform to：符合，一致

 Letter 2 Buyer's advising establishment of L/C

Dear Sirs，

　　We have instructed the Bank of Boston, Massachusetts, U. S. A to open an irrevocable letter of credit for USD 28,000 in your favor, valid until 28th February.

　　The documents required for negotiation are：

　　Commercial Invoice in duplicate；

　　Bills of Lading in triplicate；

　　Insurance Policy in one original and three copies.

　　Please make sure that the shipment is effected within April, since prompt delivery is one of the important considerations in dealing with our market.

　　We are looking forward to your shipping advice.

　　　　　　　　　　　　　　　　　　　　　　　　　Yours sincerely，

　　　　　　　　　　　　　　　　　　　　　　　　　Alex

 **Notes**

1. We have instructed. . . Bank. . . to open an irrevocable letter of credit for. . . in your favor, valid until. . . ：我方已通知……银行开立以贵方为受益人的不可撤销信用证，金额为……，有效期至……

2. negotiation：议付

3. Commercial Invoice in duplicate：商业发票一式两份

4. Bills of Lading in triplicate：提单一式三份

5. Insurance Policy in one original and three copies：保单一份正本、三份副本

6. prompt delivery：及时交货

7. shipping advice：装船通知

Letter 3   Asking for the amendment of L/C

Dear Sirs，

　　We have received your L/C No. PY9118 covering your order No. 775.

　　After checking，we found some discrepancies. Please make the following necessary amendments without delay：

　　(1)Increase the amount of your L/C by USD520.

　　(2)Allow partial shipment and transshipment and delete the clause "by direct steamer".

　　(3)Amend the quantity to read：8,000 M/T (3％ more or less at seller's option).

　　Please see to it that your amendment advice reach us by 15th March，otherwise shipment will be further delayed.

　　　　　　　　　　　　　　　　　　　　　　　　　　　Yours sincerely，

　　　　　　　　　　　　　　　　　　　　　　　　　　　Jackie

 **Notes**

　　1. ... covering your order No. . . .：关于贵方第……号订单的

　　2. discrepancies：*n.* 不符之处、差异

　　3. (to) make the following necessary amendments：做出下列必要的修改

　　4. partial shipment：分批装运、分装、分运

　　5. transshipment：转运、转船

　　6. direct steamer：直轮、直达船只

　　7. (to) amend the quantity to read：修改数量(条款)为……

　　8. 3％ more or less at seller's option：3％的溢短条款，由卖方决定

　　9. amendment advice：修改通知书

 Letter 4   Asking for the extending of L/C

Dear Mr. Steven，

　　We have received your L/C No. 228 and thank you for your cooperation.

　　We regret that we could not ship the goods by the end of July because of the delay of your L/C. We are aware that the only vessel available this month that will leave in one or two days and the deadline for booking space has passed.

　　We could ask that you extend the shipping date and credit validity for one month respectively. Please reply as soon as possible.

　　　　　　　　　　　　　　　　　　　　　　　　　　　Yours sincerely，

　　　　　　　　　　　　　　　　　　　　　　　　　　　Lily

 **Notes**

　　1. We regret that we could not ship the goods by the end of July because of the delay of

your L/C. 很抱歉,由于贵方信用证的延误,我方无法在七月底装运货物。

　　2. vessel:*n.* 船、货轮

　　3. deadline:*n.* 截止日期

　　4. booking space:订舱位

　　5. We could ask that you extend the shipping date and credit validity for one month respectively. 我方想请贵方将装运期和信用证有效期分别延长一个月。

　　extend:*v.* 延长、延期、展延

　　to extend the L/C

　　extension:*n.* 延长、延期、展延

　　the extension of the L/C

7.3　Writing Steps and Tips

Based on the above specimen letters,some essential writing steps and tips about business letters talking about terms of payment can be clearly and accurately summed up into the following aspects:

　　1. A Letter of Terms of Payment(说明支付方式的信函)

Writing steps	Examples of expressions
(1)Stating that the relevant L/C hasn't been received 感谢对方订购货物或来函	Thank you for your Order No. ... Thank you for your letter of...
(2)Stating the reason or importance for issuing the L/C in time 指出我方所要求的支付方式 (不同支付方式的不同表达方法)	Our usual terms of payment are by a confirmed, irrevocable letter of credit in our favor available by draft at sight. Most of our suppliers are drawing on us at 30 days D/P...
(3)Hoping for receiving the L/C earlier 表达与对方合作及早日收到回复的愿望	Your early reply is appreciated. We look forward to your favorable reply.

　　2. A Letter of Urging Establishment of L/C(催开信用证的信函)

Writing steps	Examples of expressions
(1)Stating that the relevant L/C hasn't been received 提醒买方货已备妥待运或交货期临近,但尚未收到相关信用证	The date of delivery is approaching, but we still have not received your L/C. The goods have been ready for shipment for quite a long time, but up to now we have not received your relative L/C.

Writing steps	Examples of expressions
(2) Stating the reason or importance for issuing the L/C in time 向对方说明需要及时开证的原因或重要性，并催促对方尽快开证	We must point out that unless your L/C reaches us by the end of this month, we shall not be able to effect shipment within the stipulated time limit. In order to book the shipping space at an earlier date, please open the L/C immediately.
(3) Hoping for receiving the L/C earlier 期望早日收到相关信用证	We wish to receive the relevant L/C at an early date.

3. A Letter of Advising the Seller of the Establishment of L/C（通知卖方信用证已开立的信函）

Writing steps	Examples of expressions
(1) Stating the contract signed or the goods under the contract signed 提及相关合同或合同项下的货物	Referring to 9,000 pieces of Men's Cotton Shirts under the Sales Contract No. ... With reference to our Contract No. ...
(2) Stating the relative L/C has been issued by the bank, mentioning the major clauses of L/C 告诉对方你方已向银行开出信用证，并提及信用证的一些主要内容	We have issued the L/C No. ... in your favor for the amount of GBP 256,000.00 through the Bank of China. The relative L/C has already been established.
(3) Hoping for effecting shipment at an early date 希望对方早日安排装运	Please inform us when the goods are shipped. Please arrange shipment immediately as per the contracted date upon receipt of the relevant L/C.

4. A Letter of Asking for the Amendment or Extending of L/C（信用证修改和展期的信函）

Writing steps	Examples of expressions
(1) Stating that the relevant L/C has been received 告诉对方已经收到信用证	We have received your L/C No. ... under the Sales Contract No. ... The L/C No. ... covering your Order No. ... has been received.

Writing steps	Examples of expressions
(2)Stating terms that do not conform to the contract and requesting amendment，or the reason for the extending of L/C 指出信用证与合同不符而需要修改的地方，或者说明展期的原因	Much to our regret，we find that the following three points do not conform to the contract. Please extend by fax the shipment date and the validity of your L/C to 20 May and 15 June respectively，thus enabling us to effect shipment of the goods.
(3)Expressing the hope for one's cooperation 希望对方给予合作	Your compliance with our request will be highly appreciated. (如蒙同意,不胜感激。) We will be unable to ship the goods in time if the amendment advice to the L/C comes too late.

7.4　Useful Expressions on Terms of Payment

1. Our terms of payment are by a confirmed，irrevocable letter of credit payable by draft at sight.

我方的支付方式是以保兑的、不可撤销的、凭即期汇票支付的信用证。

2. We only accept L/C with new customers like you.

对于像您这样的新客户，我们只接受信用证付款。

3. We are preparing to accept payment for your trial order on D/P basis.

对贵方这批试订货物，我方准备接受付款交单的支付方式。

4. In compliance with your request，we exceptionally accept delivery against D/P at sight，but this should not be regarded as a precedent.

应贵方要求，我方破例接受即期付款交单，但只此一次，下不为例。

5. Upon receipt of the above-mentioned L/C，please arrange shipment immediately as per the contracted date.

收到信用证后，请立即按合同规定的日期安排装运。

6. Much to our regret，we haven't received your letter of credit against our S/C No. 778，although it should have reached us by the end of June，as stipulated.

非常遗憾，我方尚未收到贵方第778号销售确认书项下的有关信用证，按规定它本应在6月底到达我方。

7. If your L/C fails to reach us by the end of July，we will be forced to cancel your order.

如果信用证不能在7月底前开到我处，我方将被迫撤销订货。

8. Please expedite the L/C so that we may execute the order smoothly.

请加速开出信用证，以便顺利执行订单。

9. We regret that we are unable to consider your request for payment under D/A terms.

对于贵方要求以承兑交单付款一事,我方抱歉难以考虑。

10. In order to conclude the business, we hope you will meet the half way. What about 50% by L/C and the balance by D/P?

为了做成这批生意,希望双方都各让步一半。百分之五十以信用证付款,百分之五十按付款交单怎么样?

11. To our regret, we find that the following five points in the L/C do not conform to the contract.

很遗憾,我方发现信用证条款中以下5点与合同不符。

12. Please amend the L/C to read "partial shipments and transshipment allowed".

请把信用证修改为"允许分批装运和转船"。

13. Please delete from the L/C the clause "All bank commissions and charges are for beneficiary's account".

请从信用证中删去此条款"所有银行佣金和费用由受益人支付"。

14. Please extend by fax the shipment date and the validity of your L/C to May 15th and June 2nd respectively, thus enabling us to effect shipment of the goods.

请用传真将信用证的装运期和有效期分别延长至5月15日和6月2日,以便使我方能发运货物。

15. We shall be much appreciated if you will give us a little more time to settle your account due 16th May.

对5月16日应付款项,如果能延些时间,我将非常感谢。

16. We may accept deferred payment if the quantity is over 10,000 pieces.

如数量超过1千件,我方可接受延期付款。

17. In order to save a lot of expenses on opening the L/C, we will remit you the full amount by T/T when the goods purchased by us are ready for shipment and the freight space is booked.

为了节省大量开立信用证的费用,我方将在所订购的货物已备妥待运、舱位已定下时,电汇全部金额。

18. You are kindly appreciated to see to it that punctual delivery is made within the validity of the L/C.

恳请务必在信用证有效期内按时装运。

19. Please send your remittance to our account No. 0864732509 with the Bank of China Shanghai Branch in favor of PY Iron Industries Ltd.

请将贵方汇款寄到中国银行上海分行我方0864732509账户上,受益人是PY Iron Industries Ltd。

20. In order to avoid subsequent amendment, please see to it that the L/C stipulations are in exact accordance with the terms of the Contract.

为了避免往后的修改,请务必做到信用证的规定须与合同的条款完全一致。

7.5　Exercises

Ⅰ. Translate the following terms and expressions into English.

1. 不可撤销信用证　　　2. 托收　　　　　3. 汇付

4. 电汇　　　　　　　　5. 信汇　　　　　6. 票汇

7. 付款交单　　　　　　8. 承兑交单　　　9. 现金付款

10. 分期付款　　　　　11. 延期付款　　　12. 预付货款

13. 付款定金　　　　　14. 赊账　　　　　15. 支付方式

Ⅱ. Translate the following sentences into English.

1. 贵方 F789 号订单项下金额 182000 美元的 DQ206 号信用证已收到。

2. 我方要求贵方尽快开立信用证,以便我方装货于 16 日开往西雅图的"中国"号货轮上。

3. 我方已按通常的付款条件,向贵方开立 90 天期汇票,并将汇票和装运单据一并交给我方银行。

4. 请注意信用证的规定要与合同条款完全一致,以避免后续的改证。

5. 为促成这笔交易,我方准备接受 50％用信用证,余额部分用即期付款交单方式支付。

Ⅲ. Translate the following sentences into Chinese.

1. In order to book the shipping space at an earlier date, please open the L/C immediately.

2. We only accept payment by confirmed, irrevocable L/C available by draft at sight instead of T/T reimbursement.

3. Please amend the amount of the L/C to read "2％ more or less".

4. We have issued a confirmed irrevocable letter of credit covering our Order No. 52.

5. We are pleased to inform you that your draft No. 852 has been duly honored on maturity.

Ⅳ. Writing practice.

Draft a letter according to the following points.

Suppose you are the sales manager of Fujian Southeastern Trading Co. Ltd. and have concluded business for Women's Cotton Shirts in size 155-170cm with one of the customers in Spain. When you received the L/C No. GB1-347, you found some clauses in the L/C did not conform to the contracted terms. Now write a letter asking for amendments including the following:

(1) The amount should be "USD264853.10" instead of "USD264583.10".

(2) Transshipment should be allowed.

Chapter 8   Packing

Learning objectives

To know about the importance of packing.

To understand the category of packing.

To understand transport packing marks.

To master the steps of writing letters about packing issues.

To master the useful words and expressions used in letters about packing issues.

8.1   Brief Introduction

Packing is of great significance in international trade. It is said that packing is to goods just like clothing is to human. The function of packing is to keep the goods in perfect condition with nothing lost during the process of transportation. In foreign trade, good packing is not only helpful in transporting, storing, loading and unloading goods, but also promoting sales. Except bulk goods and nude goods, most goods need packing.

1. The Categories of Packing

Generally speaking, packing can be classified into three types: sales packing, grouped packing and transport packing.

Sales packing, usually called as inner packing or primary packing, refers to packaging which constitutes a sales unit to the final user or consumer at the point of purchase. It can be designed in various forms, colors and materials, in order to be attractive to the consumers and promote sales. For example, a box which contains chocolate.

Grouped packing, also regarded as secondary packing, is that which usually constitutes a grouping of a certain number of sales units. It can be removed from the product without affecting its characteristics. For example, a cardboard containing a number of boxes of chocolate.

Transport packing is also called as outer packing, which means packaging designed to facilitate handling and transporting a number of sales units or grouped packing. Its goal is to ensure the safety and completeness of goods, while avoiding any forms of damage or missing. Outer packing must be solid enough to stand the roughest transportation and toughest conditions. And also it must be convenient to handle, store, load and unload. For example, a pallet and shrink wrap used to transport a number of cardboard containing boxes of chocolate.

2. Transport Packing Marks

Generally speaking, transport packing should be obviously marked. Transport packing marks mainly include shipping marks (also called transport marks), directive marks and warning marks.

Shipping marks are convenient for identifying, transporting and storing goods.

Shipping marks consist of:

(1)Consignor's or consignee's code name and the simple geometric figures, such as diamonds, triangles and so on;

(2)Number of the contract or the L/C;

(3)The port of the destination;

(4)Numbers of the packed goods;

(5)Weight and dimensions.

For example:

Directive marks are simple figures and concise instructions about manner of proper handling, storing, loading and unloading the packed goods. For example:

USE NO HOOKS	请勿用钩
HANDLE WITH CARE	小心轻放
THIS SIDE UP	此面朝上
FRAGILE	易碎品
KEEP DRY	保持干燥
CAUTION AGAINST WET	请勿受潮
PERISHABLE	易腐货物
NO DROPPING	切勿坠落
KEEP COOL	放置冷处
OPEN HERE	此处开取
SLING HERE	此处吊索

Warning marks are symbols or words to warn people against the hidden danger of inflammables, explosive and poisonous products. For example:

EXPLOSIVE	易爆货物
INFLAMMABLE	易燃货物
HAZARDOUS ARTICLE	危险物品
RADIOACTIVE	放射性物品
COMPRESSED GAS	压缩气体
OXIDIZING MATERIAL	氧化物

CORROSIVE   腐蚀品

8.2   Specimen Letters

 **Letter** 1

10th June，2016

China National Import & Export Corp.

Shanghai Brach

Shanghai China

Dear Sirs

S/C No. 90SP-24975

We acknowledge receipt of your letter dated the 3rd inst. enclosing the above sales contract in duplicate but wish to state that after going through the contract we find that the packing clause in it is not clear enough. The relative clause read as follows：

Packing：Seaworthy export packing，suitable for long distance ocean transportation.

In order to eliminate possible future trouble，we would like to make clear beforehand our packing requirements as follows.

The tea under the captioned contract should be packed in international standard tea boxes，24 boxes on a pallet，10 pallets in an FCL container. On the outer packing please mark our initials SCC in a diamond，under which the port of destination and our order number should be stenciled. In addition，warning marks like KEEP DRY, USE NO HOOK，etc. should also be indicated.

We have made a footnote on the contract to that effect and are returning herein one copy of the contract after duly countersigning it. We hope you will find it in order and pay special attention to the packing.

We look forward to receiving your shipping advice and thank you in advance.

Yours faithfully,

Smith，Cooper & Co.

 **Notes**

1. clause：*n.* 条款
2. read：*v.* 写明，写着
3. seaworthy：*adj.* 适合海洋运输的
4. eliminate：*v.* 消除；除去
5. trouble：*n.* 麻烦
6. beforehand：*adv.* 事先，预先
7. pallet：*n.* 托盘，小货盘

8. FCL：＝ Full Container Load,一整集装箱

9. warning marks:警告性标记

10. initial:*n.* 首字母

11. diamond:*n.* 菱形

12. port:*n.* 港口

13. destination:*n.* 目的地

14. stencil:*v.* 用模板印刷(文字或花样)

15. Keep Dry:保持干燥

16. Use No Hook:切勿用钩

17. footnote:*n.* 脚注

18. herein:*adv.* 在此,此中

19. countersign:*n.* ; *v.* 副签

20. in order:整齐

21. shipping advice:装运通知

22. We acknowledge receipt of your letter dated the 3rd inst. enclosing the above sales contract in duplicate... 我们确认收到你本月 3 日的来信,及所附上述销售合同一式两份。

acknowledge 确认。在确认对方来信时常用此词。

confirm 也是"确认"的意思,但外贸习惯上仅用在确认来往电报及电传上。

dated 是过去分词,即 which is dated... ,which 指 letter。

enclosing 是现在分词,修饰 letter,也相当于 which encloses...

inst. (instant)本月

ult. (ultimo) 上月

prox. (proximo) 下月

应该尽量避免使用这些词,使用具体的月份更为清楚。

23. The tea under the captioned contract should be packed in international standard tea boxes, 24 boxes on a pallet, 10 pallets in an FCL container. 标题合同项下的茶叶应该用国际标准茶叶纸箱,24 纸箱装一托盘,10 托盘装一集装箱(整箱)。

The tea under the captioned contract should be packed in international standard tea boxes... 本句是被动语态,说明茶叶应如何包装。

in international standard tea boxes, 24 boxes on a pallet, 10 pallets in an FCL container 作状语用,说明包装的条件。

24. our initials SCC in a diamond:菱形内刷我公司开头字母 SCC

Initial 多指姓名及公司名称的第一个字母。

25. under which the port of destination and our order number should be stenciled:其下应刷目的港及我订单号

under which 中的 which 指菱形,under 是介词。在外贸函电中前可用各种介词,如:

(1)We are sending you a contract against which we promise to sell 10 tons of fertilizer. 我们寄上合同一份,根据此合同,我们同意出售 10 吨肥料。

(2)We have received your letter of the 21st January from which we learn that you consider our price unacceptable. 我们收到你 3 月 1 日函, 你在该函中告知我, 你已经从他处满足你方要货。

(3) We have received your sample, the quality of which is found to be not up to the standard. 我们收到你方样品, 发现其质量未达到标准。

此外, 如 for、at、among 等介词可加在 which 前使用。

**Letter** 2

Dear Sirs,

Your shipment of 1,000 c/s Tinned Goods ex s. s. "Changchun" under Contract No. JB-558 has arrived at our end safely and in good condition.

The goods are found to be of excellent quality, while the packing is only middling, having a certain leeway to make up. You will understand that with many brands of the same commodity competing for sale here, merchandise is forced not only to give value but to be seen to give value.

Yours faithfully,

(Signature)

**Notes**

1. tinned goods: 罐头食品

2. ex prep. : 从……, 在……

The goods ex s. s. "Wuxi" have been re-inspected. 由"无锡"轮运来的货物已经复检。

The price is $150 per ton ex warehouse London. 在伦敦仓库外交货每吨价格是 150 美元。

在谈判由某轮运来的货物时, 多用介词 ex; 在谈判由某轮运走的货物时, 多用介词 per; by 是指由某轮承运。

We find the goods shipped ex s. s. "Manchester" satisfactory. 由"曼彻斯特"轮运来的货物令人满意。

3. in sound condition: 状况良好

in perfect condition 和 in good condition 也表示"状况良好"。

The goods arrived in good condition. 货物到达时情况良好。

4. packing is middling 包装平平常常

常用包装物有:

fiber board case	纤维板箱
veneer case	胶合板箱
kraft paper bag	牛皮纸袋
plywood case	三合板箱
polyethylene bag	聚乙烯袋
jute bag/gunny bag	黄麻袋
wooden case	木箱

skeleton case　　　　　　漏孔箱

5. leeway：*n.* 差距、余地

There is a good deal of leeway to make up. 差距较大，需要弥补。

6. Merchandise is forced not only to give value but to be seen to give value. 商品不仅要给人以价值，而且要被视为给人价值。

**Letter** 3

Dear Sirs，

　　We returned for your file the countersigned copy of Contract No. DG-5081 on September 15.

　　Please mark the bales with our initials SCC in a diamond，under which come the destination Bremen with order number 4424 below again.

　　This is to apply to all orders unless otherwise special.

Yours faithfully，

(Signature)

**Notes**

1. for your file：供贵方存档

2. the countersigned copy of Contract：已回签的合同副本

3. Please mark the bales with our initials SCC. 请在包上刷上我公司名称缩写 SCC。

4. This is to apply to all orders unless otherwise special. 上述唛头方法，除非另有规定，适用于所有订货。

5. 有关唛头的常用表达：

triangle	三角形
ABC in a diamond	菱形内 ABC
circle	圆形
rectangle	长方形
hexagon	正三角形
cross	十字形
downward triangle	倒三角形
star	星行
square	正方形
heart	心形
oval	椭圆形

Letter 4

Dear Sirs，

Re：Our Order 124

Please pack the captioned machine in a strong wooden case and wrap and pad generously all polished parts of the machines to avoid scratches and knocks against the container.

Also，please put the machine in a case of about 10 cubic meters covered with waterproof cloth and strapped vertically and horizontally with metal bands and cut vent holes in the case to minimize condensation.

Thank you for your sincere cooperation.

Yours faithfully，
(Signature)

Notes

1. Please pack the captioned machine in a strong wooden case and wrap and pad generously all polished parts of the machines to avoid scratches and knocks against the container. 请用结实的木箱包装这个机器，并将该机器的所有光亮部件全部充分地包裹起来，并加充足的衬塞，以避免与集装箱碰撞，导致划痕和碰伤印。

2. in a strong wooden case：用坚固的木箱

3. wrap：*v.* 包裹

4. pad：*v.* 给······加垫子

5. scratch：*n.* 擦痕，刮痕

6. knock：*n.* 碰、撞

7. generously：*adv.* 丰富地，大量地，充足地

8. cubic meter：立方米

9. Also，please put the machine in a case of about 10 cubic meters covered with waterproof cloth and strapped vertically and horizontally with metal bands and cut vent holes in the case to minimize condensation.

这个句子的主干很简单，就是"Also please put the machine in a case and cut vent holes"，意思是"请把这台机器放在······的(木)箱里，并在(木)箱上打通风孔······"。

这个句子的修饰语却很复杂。一方面，有由介词 of 和 with 引导的介词性短语做后置定语，如 of about 10 cubic meters(约 10 立方米)，covered with waterproof cloth (用防水布覆盖)，strapped vertically and horizontally with metal bands(用金属带垂直水平地箍紧)；另一方面，还有由不定式 to 引导的目的性状语 to minimize condensation(以减少冷凝作用)。

8.3　Writing Steps and Tips

Based on the above specimen letters，some essential writing steps and tips about business letters about packing issues can be summed up into the following points.

1. A Letter Informing Packing Requirements（说明包装方式的信函）

Writing steps	Examples of expressions
(1)Stating the writing purpose，that is，the discussion about packing conditions 告知对方写信的目的(关于包装问题的洽谈)	To eliminate possible future trouble, we would like to make clear beforehand our packing requirements as follows.
(2)Stating the detailed packing requirements including packing manners，packing materials，etc. 说明包装方式、包装材料等包装要求	Please be informed that for your future orders we shall pack our garments in cartons instead of in wooden cases, as packing in cartons has the following advantages.
(3)Stating the hope for one's acceptance for the packing requirements and an earlier reply 希望对方能接受你方包装的要求，并盼早日回复	Meanwhile, we wish to know the details of the packing of your lotus nuts, i. e. what measures will you take to prevent the inner packing from being torn apart?

2. A Letter Replying to a Packing Letter（回复包装的信函）

Writing steps	Examples of expressions
(1)Stating the receipt of the letter of packing requirements. 包装信函已经收悉	Thank you for your packing instructions. We have received your letter about packing requirements.
(2)Stating the opinions about the packing requirements. a)If agree, confirm the details about packing； b) If disagree, give the reason and suggestion about packing 告知是否同意对方的包装要求。 如同意,可确认一下包装的细节;如不同意,要陈述理由并提出修改建议	We are ready to accept your packing requirements and now confirm the details as follows. We regret to inform you that we cannot accept your packing requirements, because... To..., we would like to recommend you our latest package as follows. We shall pack... in... instead of in...
(3)Hoping for receiving a reply earlier 希望得到对方的尽早回复	We are expecting your confirmation on the packing at an early date. Your early confirmation on our packing solution is highly appreciated.

8.4　Useful Expressions on Packing

1. Since then we have improved the old mode of packing with the result that our recent shipments have all turned out to the full satisfaction of our customers.

此后,我们改进了老式包装,结果表明我们的客户对近几批货物完全满意。

2. In gunny bags of 60 kgs. net each.

用黄麻袋包装,每袋净重 60 千克。

3. Each carton is lined with a polythene sheet and secured by overall iron strapping, thus preventing the contents from dampness and possible damage through rough handling.

每一纸板箱衬以塑料纸,全箱用铁箍加固,以防内装货物受潮及因粗暴搬运而可能引起的损坏。

4. Our usual packing is in wooden cases of 112 lbs. net，each containing 16 packets of 7 lbs.

我们通常用木箱装,每箱的净重是 112 磅,每箱装 16 纸盒,每纸盒的净重是 7 磅。

5. Pliers are packed 2 dozen to a box and 100 boxes to a wooden case.

钳子两打装一盒,一百盒装一木箱。

6. Packing in sturdy wooden cases is essential. Cases must be nailed，battened and secured by overall metal strapping.

必须要使用坚固的木箱,箱体要用铁钉订牢,整体用木板和金属条封好。

7. We shall pack the goods in our usual packing if you have nothing particular in this regard.

如果你在这一点上没有特殊要求,我们将采用惯常包装。

8. Usual Packing:25kg drum with inner plastic bag.

一般包装:25 千克桶,内衬塑料袋。

9. The cartons are well protected against moisture by polythene sheet lining.

这些纸板箱内衬聚乙烯纸,防潮效果好。

10. The cigars are packed 5 pieces to a small packet，20 packets to a carton,144 cartons to a cardboard container.

雪茄 5 只一小包装,20 包一箱,144 箱一纸板箱。

11. The goods we packed in new and sound jute bags, each containing about 200 pounds.

我们将货物装进新而结实的麻袋里,每袋 200 磅。

12. All the goods will be packed according to the special way you require.

所有货物根据你方要求的方式包装。

13. If the goods are packed in cartons, any traces of pilferage will be in evidence, therefore the insurance company may be made to pay the necessary compensation for such losses.

如果用纸箱包装,任何偷窃痕迹都很明显,因此保险公司很易做出赔偿。

14. Our packing is strong enough to withstand bumping and rough handling under normal conditions.

我们的包装足够坚固,正常情况下经得起碰撞和野蛮搬装运。

15. The export cases used to pack the goods are strong enough to protect the instruments.

包装用的出口木箱坚固,足以保护设备。

16. Our strip scissors are packed in boxes of one dozen each，200 boxes to a wooden case.

我们的磨剪一打一盒,200 盒一木箱。

17. The packing of our mens shirts is each in a polybag, 5 dozen to a carton lined with waterproof paper and bound with two iron straps outside.

我们男式衬衫的包装为每一个聚乙烯袋一件,5 打一纸箱,内衬防水纸,外加两条铁带加固。

18. We plan to use cardboard or plastic cartons for the outer packing.

我们计划用纸板或塑料箱作为外包装。

19. The cases used for packing our transistor radios are light but strong.

我们电子收音机包装用的木箱轻巧、坚固。

20. We regret to learn your satisfaction with the packing for the last shipment but we can assure you of our special attention to the packing of your future shipments.

得知贵方对我们上批货的包装不满意,我们深表遗憾。但是,我们可以向贵方保证,以后一定特别注意货物的包装。

8.5 Exercises

Ⅰ. Fill in the blank with the following words and expressions.

transportation	push	packed	expenses	suitable
protected	effected	inner	attractive	secured

1. We usually have our Screws _____ in double gunny bags of 60 kgs. each.

2. The cartons are well _____ against moisture by polythene sheet lining.

3. We can meet your special requirements for packing but the extra _____ should be borne by you.

4. As it will take us time to pack the goods according to your requirements，we are afraid that the shipment may be _____ at the contracted time.

5. The goods ordered should be of good quality and in _____ packing.

6. All bags have an _____ waterproof lining.

7. When the various products ordered by you are complete in our warehouse，we will pack them into bundles of _____ size for shipment.

8. We do not object to packing in cartons, provided the flaps are glued down and the cartons _____ by metal bands.

9. Our improved packing will catch the eye of the buying public, which will help _____ the sales.

10. Our cartons are strong enough to stand rough handling in the course of _____.

Ⅱ. Translate the following terms and expressions from Chinese into English or from English into Chinese.

1. 外包装

2. 销售装

3. 唛头

4. 一整集装箱

5. 习惯包装

6. directive marks

7. warning marks

8. stencil

9. Use No Hook

10. Keep Dry

Ⅲ. Translate the following sentences into Chinese.

1. We have examined the polythene bag you sent us and find it acceptable if you could o-mit the brand name on the bag as agreed before.

2. Please see to it that straws are not allowed here as filling material.

3. We appreciate the quality of your Alarm Clocks but should like to know how they are packed.

4. We have adopted carton packing instead of wooden cases as the former is just as sea-worthy as the latter while the cost is less and the weight lighter.

5. Our Soya Beans are supplied in bulk or in gunny bags.

6. Our cotton prints are packed in cases lined with draft paper and waterproof paper, each consisting of 30 pieces with 5 colors for on design.

Ⅳ. Translate the following sentences into English.

1. 我们能按你们的要求用木箱装货,但你们要承担额外的包装费。(extra packing charge)

2. 请对包装特别注意,否则,货物将在运输途中损毁。(special attention)

3. 若能提供小包装,那就更好了。(small packing)

4. 在我们商品的塑料袋上及纸盒上都印有商品的图样,这样就能帮助客户了解他正在买的商品。(sample)

5. 包装需符合我地市场爱好。(preference)

6. 对你方指定的包装,我们要收取费用,因为这需要额外的劳力及成本。(designated packing)

Ⅴ. Write a letter about packing issues according to the following requirements.

我方订单号为 S957 的货物在包装时应注意以下几个方面:

(1)包装能够防止偷盗;

(2)包装适合海洋运输;

(3)包装的防潮效果要好;

(4)包装要能经受运输途中的恶劣条件及粗暴操作。

期待按时收到货物,并保证货物质量优良,包装完整无损,不影响销售。

Chapter 9　Insurance

Learning objectives

　　To know the relevant parties and coverage of marine insurance.

　　To grasp the structure of a letter related to the arrangement of insurance.

　　To know how to make a claim for the insured cargoes.

　　To master the useful words and expressions on marine insurance.

9.1　Brief Introduction

According to the different types of subject matter insured, insurance can be classified into four kinds: property insurance, product liability insurance, export credit insurance and life insurance. Marine insurance is a kind of property insurance which provides a guarantee for the cargoes in marine transportation.

The insurance company is the insurer who can provide protection for the insured cargoes. In China, the People's Insurance Company of China (PICC) established in 1949 is a comprehensive state-owned insurance company and one of the biggest insurance companies in the world. The insured is the one who buys insurance from the insurance company and searches for protection from the latter.

The insurance premium is the amount of money given by the insured to the insurance company, and the insurance value is the highest compensation that the insurance company shall pay. Usually, the insurance value covers the CIF or CIP price plus a certain percentage of addition as market profits, and premium is calculated based on the insurance value.

Insurance policy is the document or contract between the insurer and the insured. It contains all the information about the goods, coverage, the insurance value, premium and the obligations of each party (see appendix 1).

Chinese import or export companies mainly adopt the China Insurance Clauses (C.I.C.) stipulated by PICC for cargo insurance. C.I.C consists of two parts: basic coverage and additional coverage. Basic coverage is of three kinds: FPA, WPA and All Risks.

FPA is an abbreviation for free from particular average. It provides the coverage for the total loss, average loss and particular loss only caused by accidents, or particular loss caused by both natural disasters and accidents. However, it excludes the particular loss only caused by natural disasters.

WPA means with particular average. It includes the coverage of FPA and particular loss caused by natural disasters, such as lightening, storm, earthquake, flood and so on. So it provides a wider range of protection than FPA.

All Risks include the coverage of WPA and the general additional risks, such as TPND (theft, Pilferage and Non-delivery), fresh water rain damage, risk of odor and so on. But All Risks exclude the special additional risks, such as war risk and strike risks. Such special additional risks shall be covered together with the basic coverage.

Different from China Insurance Clause proposed by PICC, Institute of London Underwriters (I. L. U.) stipulated Institute Cargo Clauses (I. C. C.) in 1982 which have a far influence on the global trade. ICC is made up of six parts, ICC(A), ICC(B), ICC(C), Institute War Clauses-Cargo, Institute Strikes Clauses-Cargo, and Malicious Damage Clauses. The previous five types can be covered alone, but the six risks shall be covered together with the other risks. ICC (A) is similar to Chinese All risks, ICC (B) is equivalent to Chinese WPA, and ICC(C) is like Chinese FPA with some small distinctions.

When the importer or exporter purchases insurance, he or she shall take full consideration of the following factors: the characteristics of the cargoes, the condition of the packages, the modes of transportation, the political situation of the destination country and so on.

When the insured is informed of the losses of or damage to the goods, he or she shall promptly notify the insurer so that the latter can survey the event, put forward the rescuing suggestions and define the liabilities of relevant party. Sometimes, if the carriers, stevedoring companies or the customs are involved in the losses or damage, they shall reimburse the insured.

In writing letters talking about insurance, the following points may be included:

a. The consignment to be insured;

b. The insurance to be covered by whom;

c. The risks to be covered;

d. The insurance value;

e. The premium and etc.

9.2   Specimen Letters

 Letter 1   Seller enquiring about the insurance

Dear Sir,

Please quote your rate for all risks open policy for US $ 15.000 to cover shipments of general merchandise by Southeast Asia Shipping Line from Singapore to Atlantic ports in Canada and the United States. Any shipments are due to begin on 21st April, please let us have your quotation by return.

Sincerely yours,

 **Notes**

1. quote:*v.* ~(sth.)引用,报价,

quotation *n.* 估价,报价

He's always quoting verses from the Bible. 他总是引用圣经中的诗句。

This is the best price I can quote you. 这是我能报的最优价。

The insurance company requires three quotations for repairs to the car. 保险公司需要三份修理汽车的报价单。

2. all risks:一切险

中国人民保险公司制定的中的国保险条款中三大主险:All Risks 一切险,WPA 水渍险,FPA 平安险。

3. open policy:预约保单。它载明保险货物的范围、承保险别、保险费率、每批运输货物的最高保险金额以及保险费的计算办法。凡属于预约保单的保范围内的进出口货物,一经起运,即自动按预约保单所列条件承保,但被保险人在获悉每批货物起运时,应立即以起运通知书或其他书面形式将该批货物的名称、数量、保险金额、运输工具的种类和名称、航程起讫地点、开航日期等情况通知保险公司。预约保单不规定承保货物的总价值,不会发生保尽的问题,它按保单规定的期限自动承保保单内的一切货运。

4. cover:*v.* ~sb. /sth. (against sth.) 给某人或某事物办理保险

Are you fully covered against fire? 你是否保了足够的火险?

cover insurance:arrange, effect, provide, take out insurance

cover insurance on (sth.) 对某货物投保

cover insurance against (risk) 投保防范的险别

cover insurance at (a certain rate of premium) 投保的费率

cover insurance with (an insurance company) 向某保险公司投保

cover insurance for (a certain amount of money) 投保金额

5. shipment:*n.* 装船,装载的货物

arrange shipment immediately 立即安排装运

a shipment of grain for West Africa 运往西非的谷物

6. general merchandise:日用商品,杂货品

7. line:(轮船、公共汽车、飞机等)运输公司

a shipping line/an airline 航运公司/空运公司.

8. due:*adj* (做表语 be due to do sth.)预定做某事,(做定语)适当的.

The train is due to arrive in five minutes. 火车将在五分钟后到达。

After due consideration, he decided to go there. 经过慎重考虑,他决定去那里。

9. by return (of post):请即回复

Please reply by return. 请尽快加回复。

Letter 2   Seller providing information on the insurance

Dear sir，

　　With reference to your letter of May 4th on inquiring about the insurance on our CIF offer for air conditioner，we'd like to provide the following information for your reference.

　　In general，we effect insurance with the People's Insurance Company of China against all risk. Should you require the insurance to be covered as per institute cargo clauses，we would be glad to do accordingly. But if the premium of the latter is higher，you will have to bear the extra premium，for which we will draw on you a clean draft. Also，you can ask for additional risks such as TPND to be included，but the additional premium will be charged your account. This insurance amount is usually 110% of the total invoice value. However if you want a higher percentage，we can comply but the extra premium is for your account as well.

　　We hope you will be satisfied with our explanation and await your decision，we remain.

　　　　　　　　　　　　　　　　　　　　　　　　　　　　Truly yours，

Notes

1. reference：*n.* 提到，涉及

With reference to：关于

e. g.：I am writing with reference to your job application.

　　我正写信提及你申请工作一事。

without reference to sb. sth：不顾

e. g.：She issued all these invitations without any reference to her superior.

　　她不顾她的上司就发出了所有这些邀请。

have no reference to sth. :与某事物无关

This has no reference to what we are discussing.

这与我们讨论的事无关。

2. inquire：*v.* 询问

inquire about：打听消息

inquire about the trains to London 询问去伦敦的火车情况

inquire after sb. :问候某人

People call to inquire after the baby.

人们打电话询问婴儿的情况。

inquire into：调查

We must inquire further into the matter.

我们必须深度调查此事。

3. CIF：全称为 cost，insurance and freight。11 个国际贸易术语之一，卖方报价由这三个部分组成。按国际贸易惯例,卖方投保的保险金额应按 CIF 价加成 10%。如买卖双方未约定具体险别,则卖方只需取得最低限底的保险险别;如买方要求加保战争保险等附加险,在保险费由买方负担的前提下,卖方应予加保。

4. Should：当从句中有 were, had 或 should 时,可省略 if,将 were, had 或 should 提到主语前,构成半倒装形式。

Should he agree to go there, we would send him there.

要是他答应去的话,我们就派他去了。

5. as per：根据

You can use online sources or books as per the requirements of your instructor.

你可以根据你的导师的要求使用在线资源或书籍。

6. premium：保险费

Your first premium is now due.

你的第一笔保险费现已到期。

7. insurance amount：保险金

8. draw on sb. ：向某人开票

9. clean draft. ：光票

光票指的是不随附任何商业单据(如货运等相关单据),而在国外付款的外币票据,种类包括:银行汇票、支票、本票(bank drafts, banker's checks, cashier's check),银行拨款单(bank money order),旅行支票(traveller's check),旅行信用证项下之汇票(drafts drawn under traveller's letter or credit),外国邮政汇票(postal money order),外国公库支票(treasury check),到期国外公债及息票(matured bonds and coupons),私人或公司行号开发之汇票、本票、支票。

10. additional risks：附加险

附加险是基本险别责任的扩大和补充,它不能单独投保。附加险包括一般附加险和特别加险。

一般附加险有 11 种,它包括:

偷窃,提货不着险(Theft, Pilferage and Non-delivery-T. P. N. D);

淡水雨淋险(Fresh Water and/or Rain Damage);

短量险(Risk of Shortage in Weight);

渗漏险(Risk of Leakage);

混杂、玷污险(Risk of Intermixture and Contamination);

碰损、破碎险(clash and breakage risks);

串味险(Risk of Odor);

受潮受热险(Sweating and Heating Risk);

钩损险(Hook Damage Risk);

包装破裂险(Breakage of Packing Risk);

锈损险(Risk of Rust)。

特殊附加险包括:

交货不到险(Failure to Deliver Risk);

进口关税险(Import Duty Risk);

舱面险(On Deck Risk);

拒收险(Rejection Risk);

黄曲霉素险(Aflatoxin Risk);

卖方利益险(Seller's Contingent Risk);

出口货物到港九或澳门存仓火险责任扩展条款(Fire Risk Extension Clause for Storage of Cargo of Destination Hong Kong Including Kowloon, or Macao);

罢工险(Strike Risk);

战争险(War Risk)。

11. invoice value:发票金额

12. insure:*v.* ～sth against sth,保险,投保

to insure one's house against fire 给某人的房子投火险

13. we remain:我们知道了,我们会记在心上的(商务信件的特殊用法)

Letter 3   A claim for cameras damaged

Dear Sir,

Subject:S. S. "Oriental Queen"

It is to notify you that we are holders of the Policy No. 3421 issued by your office for 20 cases of cameras valued HK $ 150,000 of which three of the twenty cases of cameras were damaged which are valued HK $ 12,000 as the consignment arrived at Singapore. We hereby enclose the certificate of survey and the policy which is against all risks.

We hope sincerely that you will kindly adjust the claims and settle the account at the earliest convenience.

Sincerely yours,

 Notes

1. S. S:(abbre. for steamship)轮船

2. case:木箱

3. consignment:所托运之货物,寄售物;托运,寄售

4. certificate of survey:检验报告

5. policy:保单

6. claim:*n.* 索赔

lodge, file, make, put in a claim for sth (e.g. the damages) 为……提出索赔

file a claim against sb. (e.g. seller or the insurance company) 向……提出索赔

adjust the claim (结算保险赔偿金时)评定损失应赔偿的款项

settle the claim 受理索赔

withdraw the claim 撤销索赔

9.3 Writing Steps and Tips

Based on the above specimen letters, some essential writing steps and tips about business letters of insurance can be clearly and accurately summed up into the following points.

1. The Steps of an Insurance Letter（保险信函）

Writing steps	Examples of expressions
(1) Stating your writing purpose about the insurance for the specific goods 说明写信的目的，提出想要将何种货物保险的意向	Referring to the cargo under S/C No. . . . We would like to insure the following consignment against. . . We are pleased to inform you that. . .
(2) Stating details and requests about the insurance, such as coverage, amount, premium, etc 陈述保险的具体细节，如投保险别、保险金额、保险费等。	Please have the goods insured against ALL RISKS for 110％ of the invoice value. We shall be appreciated if you will arrange to insure the goods on our behalf against. . . at invoice value plus. . . ％, amounting to. . . We will refund the premium to you upon receipt of your debit note.
(3) Hoping to receive the earlier reply 希望对方同意保险要求，并盼早日回复	We hope that you can arrange insurance according to our request. We are awaiting your prompt and favorable reply. We trust you will promptly settle this matter.

2. The Steps of Wring a Reply to an Insurance Letter（回复保险信函）

Writing steps	Examples of expressions
(1) Stating thanks and confirmation for the request of insurance 感谢对方关于投保的来信，并确认办理保险的要求	Thank you for your letter of April 8 requesting us to insure. . . against. . . We have received your letter asking us to handle insurance on the consignment of. . . against. . . for. . . ％ of the invoice value.
(2) Stating the detailed insurance conditions, such as carrier, coverage, amount, premium, insurance documents, etc. 详细告知保险的具体细节，如承保人、险别、金额、保费、保单等	We will cover insurance against WPA according to usual practice in the absence of definite instructions from you. The premium is at the rate of 1. 5％ of the value declared. We are glad to inform you that we have covered the insurance of the goods against FPA for. . . with. . . We will send you the insurance policy together with a debit not for the premium fee.
(3) Hoping to receive the earlier reply 希望得知对方是否同意保险条件，并盼早日回复	We hope this matter will come to your best attention. If our rate is acceptable to you, please let us know it so that our insurance policy can reach you promptly.

9.4 Useful Expressions on Insurance

1. Please insure the goods against TPND.

请投保偷窃、提货不着险。

2. Please have the goods insured against FPA for 110% of the invoice value.

请按发票金额的 110% 投保平安险。

3. Would you please cover this consignment on behalf of us against All Risks and Strike Risk for 120% of the invoice value?

贵方能否代表我方对这批货物按发票金额的 120% 投保一切险和罢工险呢?

4. We will refund the premium to you upon receipt of your debit note.

一收到贵方的还款通知,我方会立即将保险费退还贵方。

5. We require immediate cover and shall be grateful if you will let us have the policy as soon as it is ready.

我方要求尽快投保,并尽快让我们拿到保险单。

6. We have insured the cargoes with PICC against All Risks for 110% of invoice value.

我方已经将货物按发票金额的 110% 向中国人民保险公司投保一切险。

7. As usual, the goods have been insured on WAP terms.

按惯常做法,货物已保水渍险。

8. The premium for this cover is at the rate of 1% of the value declared.

这份保险的保险费率是申请投保金额的 1%。

9. We cannot grant you insurance coverage for 150% of the invoice value.

我方无法同意贵方按发票金额 150% 的投保要求。

10. Breakage is a special risk, for which an extra premium will have to be charged.

破碎险是一种特殊险别,要额外收费。

11. We usually effect insurance against ALL RISKS for the invoice value plus 10% for the goods sold on CIF basis.

我们通常按照 CIF 票面金额加 10% 投保一切险。

12. An insurance claim should be submitted to the insurance company within 30 days after the arrival of the consignment at the port of destination.

保险索赔应该在货物到达目的港的 30 天内提交保险公司。

13. Much to regret, we cannot accept this claim as you have not covered the risk of breakage.

非常遗憾,因为贵方没有投保破碎险,所以我方不能接受该索赔。

14. We will send you the insurance policy together with a debit note for the premium fee.

我方会把保险单以及保险费款的还款通知一并寄给贵方。

15. We hope we could serve your company to your satisfaction.

我方希望我们对贵公司提供的服务令贵方满意。

9.5 Exercises

Ⅰ. Translate the following terms into Chinese.

1. the insurer	2. the insured	3. insurance premium
4. insurance value	5. insurance policy	6. FPA
7. WPA	8. All Risks	9. C. I. C
10. I. C. C.	11. shipping line	12. open policy
13. by return	14. clean draft	15. additional risks
16. invoice value	17. certificate of survey	18. debit note

Ⅱ. Translate the following sentences into Chinese.

1. We shall be much pleased if you will kindly arrange to insure the same cargoes on our behalf against All Risks for 110% of the invoice value，i. e. ＄100,000.

2. The policy will be sent to you in a day or two together with our debit note for the premium.

3. The shipment should be covered WPA for 120% of the invoice value.

4. We hereby want to keep you informed that the goods will need to add War Risk at the proportion of 0.3% of the invoice value.

5. We have arranged for the surveyor to investigate the extent of the damage and shall forward his report together with our claim as soon as possible.

6. If the breakage is surveyed to be less than 7%，no claim for damage will be entertained.

Ⅲ. Translate the following sentences into English.

1. 如果我们以 CIF 价成交，我们将投保水渍险。

2. 如果你没有明确的指示，我们将一如既往地投保一切险。

3. 我们已为你方第 34 号订单投保了发票金额加 10% 的货到目的港。

4. 请按发票金额的 110% 投保平安险。

5. 在完成保险手续后，贵方可以向我们开出即期汇票，以便我们重新为你支付保险费。

6. 如果投保附加险，额外的费用将由贵方承担。

Ⅳ. Write a letter in English based on the information given below.

请为 1000 台"海尔"空调投保一切险，价值约为 CNY3,000,000,此货物由长江号货轮从武汉运至新加坡，7 月 15 号起航，按高出发票价值的 15% 投保，要求 PICC 保险公司告知保费，速寄来保险单。

Appendix 1 Insurance Policy

中国人民保险公司

The People's Insurance Company of China

货物运输保险单

CARGOES TRANSPORTATION INSURANCE POLICY

发票号(INVOICE NO.)

合同号(CONTRACT NO.)

信用证号(L/C NO.)

被保险人：

INSURED：

保单号次

POLICY NO.

中国人民保险公司(以下简称本公司)根据被保险人的要求,由被保险人向本公司缴付约定的保险费,按照本保险单承保险别和背面所载条款与下列特款承保下述货物运输保险,特立本保险单。

THIS POLICY OF INSURANCE WITNESSES THAT THE PEOPLE'S INSURANCE COMPANY OF CHINA (HEREINAFTER CALLED "THE COMPANY") AT THE REQUEST OF THE INSURED AND IN CONSIDERATION OF THE AGREED PREMIUM PAID TO THE COMPANY BY THE INSURED, UNDERTAKES TO INSURE THE UNDERMENTIONED GOODS IN TRANSPORTATION SUBJECT TO THE CONDITIONS OF THIS OF THIS POLICY AS PER THE CLAUSES PRINTED OVERLEAF AND OTHER SPECIAL CLAUSES ATTACHED HEREON.

标 记 MARKS&NOS	包装及数量 QUANTITY	保险货物项目 DESCRIPTION OF GOODS	保险金额 AMOUNT INSURED
	TOTAL		

总保险金额

TOTAL AMOUNT INSURED：_____

启运日期：   装载运输工具：

保费：

PERMIUM：____ DATE OF COMMENCEMENT：____ PER CONVEYANCE：____

自   经   至

FROM：_____ VIA _____ TO _____

承保险别：

CONDITIONS：

所保货物,如发生保险单项下可能引起索赔的损失或损坏,应立即通知本公司下述代理人查勘。如有索赔,应向本公司提交保单正本(本保险单共有 份正本)及有关文件。如一份正本已用于索赔,其余正本自动失效。

IN THE EVENT OF LOSS OR DAMAGE WITCH MAY RESULT IN A CLAIM UNDER THIS POLICY, IMMEDIATE NOTICE MUST BE GIVEN TO THE COMPANY'S AGENT AS MENTIONED HEREUNDER. CLAIMS, IF ANY, ONE OF THE ORIGINAL POLICY WHICH HAS BEEN ISSUED INORIGINAL(S)   TOGETHER WITH THE RELEVANT DOCUMENTS SHALL BE SURRENDERED TO THE COMPANY. IF ONE OF THE ORIGINAL POLICY HAS BEEN ACCOMPLISHED. THE OTHERS TO BE VOID.

中国人民保险公司

The People's Insurance Company of China

赔款偿付地点

CLAIM PAYABLE AT _____ ANDYLVKING

出单日期

ISSUING DATE _____   Authorized Signature * * * _____

Appendix 2 Open Policy

进口货物运输预约保险合同
合同号×××　　年/号×××

甲方：

乙方：中国人民保险公司

双方就进口货物的运输预约保险，议定下列各条以资共同遵守：

一、保险范围

甲方从国外进口的全部货物，不论运输方式，凡贸易条件规定由买方办理保险的，都属于合同范围之内。甲方应根据本合同规定，向乙方办理投保手续并支付保险费。

乙方对上述保险范围内的货物，负有自动承保的责任，在发生本合同规定范围内的损失时均按本合同的规定负责赔偿。

二、保险金额

保险金额以进口货物的 CIF 价为准。如果交易不是以 CIF 价成交，则折算成 CIF 价。计算时，运费可用实际运费，亦可由双方协定一个平均运费率计算。

三、保险险别和费率

各种货物需要投保的险别由甲方选定并在投保单中填明。乙方根据不同的险别，规定不同的费率。现暂定如下：

货物种类	运输方式	保险险别	保险费率
集装箱货物	海运	平安	

四、保险责任

各种险别的责任范围，以所属乙方制定的"海洋货物运输保险条款""海洋货物运输战争险条款""航空运输综合险条款"和其他有关条款的规定为准。

五、投保手续

甲方一经掌握货物发运情况，即应向乙方发出起运通知书，办理投保。通知书一式五份，由保险公司签定、确认后，退回一份。如果不办理投保，货物发生损失，乙方不予理赔。

六、保险费

乙方按甲方寄送的起运通知书照前列相应的费率逐笔计收保险费，甲方应及时付费。

七、索赔手续和期限

本合同所保货物发生保险范围以内的损失时，乙方应按制定的"关于海运进口保险货物残损检验和赔款给付办法"迅速处理。甲方应尽力采取防止货物扩大受损的措施，对已遭受损失的货物必须积极抢救，尽量减少货物的损失。向乙方办理索赔的有效期限，以保险货物卸离海轮之日起满一年终止。如有特殊需要，可向乙方提出延长索赔期。

八、合同期限

本合同自：　　年　　月　　日开始生效。

甲方：　　　　　　　　　　　乙方：中国人民保险公司

Chapter 10   Shipment

Learning objectives

To learn about shipping instructions and shipping advice.

To know the essential components of a letter of shipment.

To be able to useful words and expressions in writing a letter of shipment.

10. 1   Brief Introduction

So far, some of the previous chapters have chiefly dealt with making preparations for exporting goods before their shipment. Now is the time for the seller to deliver or ship the designated goods according to the time, place, and method of delivery or shipment agreed upon between him and the buyer. This is the basic task and obligation the exporter has to undertake while executing the sales contract. Shipment covers rather a wide range of work, such as buyers' sending shipping instructions, sellers' sending shipping advice, booking shipping space, chartering ships, appointing shipping agent, arranging shipment, nomination of vessels, etc.

In international trade, it is generally accepted that the contract is broken if the consignor (or exporter) does not dispatch the goods in accordance with the time and mode of delivery as agreed upon between the consignee (or importer) and the consignor (or exporter). Therefore, in negotiating the clause dealing with the transportation of goods in a sales contract the elements of time, types of shipping services, freight, etc. should be under careful consideration.

The shipment should come into effect neither too long nor too short a time after the contract is concluded. Generally, if the shipment is made too early, there will be insufficient time for the exporter to get the goods ready. If it is made too late, the exporter will have to wait quite a long time before he can get the payment. Or, in other words, he will be out of funds for long. The best way out is to take up a time limit that best suits his case. Generally speaking, there are three ways of setting the time of shipment:

1. The shipment with a fixed period of time

e. g. "shipment during September", "March shipment", "shipment at or before the end of June", "shipment on or before April. 20" or "shipment during Oct. /Nov. "

2. The shipment with an indefinite date

e. g. shipment within 30days after the date of receipt of the letter of credit, shipment

subject to shipping space available

3. The shipment with a date in the near future

e. g. immediate shipment, prompt shipment, shipment as soon as possible.

Letters regarding shipment are usually written for the following purposes: to urge an early shipment; to amend shipping terms; to give shipping advice; to dispatch shipping documents and so on.

10.2　Specimen Letters

 Letter 1　Shipping Instructions

Dear Sirs,

Re：S/C No. 121 Covering 3,000 Cubic Meters Timbers

We refer to your letter dated 15th this month in connection with the above subject.

In reply, we are glad to inform you that the relevant L/C No. 132 has been opened with the Bank of China, Dalian Branch for the amount of USD 18,000. Upon receipt of the same, please arrange shipment of the above as soon as possible.

We are informed by the forwarding company here that there is a direct steamer S. S. "Brook" sailing for your port on or about 2nd July. It would be appreciated if you could ship in one lot by that steamer.

Thank you in advance for your cooperation.

Yours faithfully,

 **Notes**

1. shipping instructions：装运须知

2. in connection with：与……相关

e. g. ：In connection with your enquiry of June 10, we are sorry to tell you that steel plates are unavailable at present.

关于你方 6 月 10 日的询盘,我们很抱歉地通知您目前钢板缺货。

connection：n. 客户,往来关系

e. g. ：We have business connections all over the world.

我们的客户遍布世界各地。

3. for the amount of：金额计……

4. forwarding company：货代公司

5. sail：v. 启航,开航

e. g. ：The ship is scheduled to sail for Hong Kong on the 21st of this month.

这艘船将按计划于本月 21 号驶往香港。

sailing date 启航日期

sailing port 启航港

sailing schedule 船期表

6. in one lot：一批

in two lots：两批

shipment in three equal lots：分三批等量装运

e. g. ：We prefer to ship whatever is ready instead of waiting for the completion of the entire lot.

我们愿意装运所有备妥货物，而不愿等整批货备妥再装运。

7. in advance：提前，预先

 **Letter 2   Shipping Advice**

Dear Sirs，

5. 000M/Ts Palm Oil under S/C No. 122

We are now pleased to inform you that we have shipped the above goods on board S. S. "Sea Brave" which sails for your port tomorrow.

Enclosed please find one set of shipping documents covering this consignment，which comprises：

1. One non-negotiable copy of B/L；

2. Commercial Invoice in duplicate；

3. One copy of Certificate of Quality；

4. One copy of Certificate of Origin；

5. One copy of Insurance Policy；

6. Weight Memo in duplicate.

We are glad to have been able to execute your order as contracted and trust that the goods will reach you in good time to meet your urgent need and that they will turn out to your entire satisfaction.

We trust you will be completely satisfied with the goods and look forward to your further orders.

Yours faithfully，

 **Notes**

1. on board：装上船

2. S. S. ：＝steamship，轮；号

e. g. ：We have received the captioned shipment ex S. S. "East Wing".

我方已经收到"东翼"号货轮运来的标题下货物。

3. consignment：n. 一批交付的货物；货物；委托装运的货物

e. g. ：You may sell the consignment merchandise at the prevailing price less one percent.

你们可以低于现行市价1%的价格出售这些货物。

on consignment：寄售

e. g. : She sold clothes on consignment to benefit homeless people.

他以代售方式卖服装来施益于无家可归的人。

4. B/L：＝Bill of Lading,提单

non-negotiable copy of B/L:不可转让的提单

e. g. : Unsigned Bill of Lading is non-negotiable.

未经签署的提单不可转让。

5. execute:v. 执行,类似于 carry out

e. g. : Please do your utmost to execute this order as it will lead to other business.

请尽最大努力执行这个订单,因为它将带来其他生意。

execution:执行

e. g. : We regret that the execution of the agreement is far from satisfaction.

很遗憾协议的执行远不能令人满意。

6. in good time:及时地,准时地

e. g. : Your ordered goods will reach you in good time.

你方所订货物会及时到达你处。

7. turn out:结果……

e. g. : Things turned out to be exactly as the professor had foreseen.

事情正如教授所预见的那样。

8. to your entire satisfaction:完全令你方满意

e. g. : We are sorry to learn that the goods supplied were not to your satisfaction.

我们遗憾地得知你们对所提供的货物不满意。

 Letter 3   Urging early shipment

Dear Mr. Smith,

Our Order No. 123

We are now very anxious to know about the shipment of our above order for 3,000 "Butterfly" brand sewing machines which should be delivered before March 10 as contracted.

Now the shipment date is approaching rapidly, but so far we have not received any information from you concerning this lot. When we placed the order we explicitly pointed out that punctual shipment was very important because our customers were in urgent need of the goods and we had given them assurance of an early delivery.

We hope you will make every effort to make shipment within the stipulated time as any delay would cause us no small difficulty.

Sincerely,

 **Notes**

1. contract:v. 签合同

as contracted:按合同约定

e. g. : The users are in urgent need of the machines contracted and are in fact pressing us for assurance of an early delivery.

　　　　客户们急需合同项下的机器,而且实际上正在催促我们要保证早日装船。

　　　　We have contracted with a clothing firm for 2,000 men's shirts a week.

　　　　我们已经和一家服装公司订立了合同,每周交 2000 件男士衬衫。

2. anxious:*adj.* 渴望的,急切的

e. g. : We are anxious to establish business relations with you.

　　　　我们盼望和你们建立业务关系。

3. approach:*v.* 接近,与……接触

e. g. : We approach you for importing chemicals.

　　　　我们为进口化工产品与你方接洽。

4. so far:到目前为止,类似于 up to now, up to date, up till now

e. g. : We wish to inform you that the supply of this commodity in our market has so far been monopolized by a Japanese make.

　　　　我们愿告知你方,此商品在我方市场的供应迄今为一种日本货所垄断。

5. point out:指出

e. g. : We must point out that our offer is subject to your reply reaching us before 6th June.

　　　　我们必须指出我方报盘以你方 6 月 6 日之前复到有效。

6. stipulate:*v.* 规定

e. g. : The contract stipulates that shipment be made in June.

　　　　合同规定 6 月份装运。

　　　　It is stipulated in our Sales Confirmation that payment be made by L/C.

　　　　我们的销售确认书规定用信用证付款。

7. cause:*v.* 致使,导致

e. g. : This has caused us a great loss.

　　　　这给我们造成了很大损失。

　　　　Our investigation shows that damage was caused by importer packing.

　　　　检验证明,货物受损是包装不当造成的。

8. no small difficulty:不小的困难, no small=great

e. g. : He has caused us no small trouble.

　　　　他给我们带来了不少麻烦。

 Letter 4   Requesting for transshipment and partial shipments

Dear Tony,

　　We are in receipt of your e-mail of yesterday requesting us to ship all the 5×40'HQ of Baby Joggers against Order No. 4350 in one lot in September. Unfortunately we are unable to comply with your wishes, due to the preparation of raw materials and our tough producing schedule.

As contracted, the delivery time of this order is up to October 31, 2013. If you desire earlier delivery, we can only make a partial shipment of $2\times40'$ HQ in September and the remaining in October, 2013. This would speed matters up if we could ship immediately the goods we have in stock instead of waiting for the whole shipment to be completed.

At present, we are advised by the forwarder that because direct vessels, either liner or tramp, sailing for Liverpool, are infrequent, and the shipping space has been fully booked up to the end of December. In the circumstances, we have to ship via Hong Kong more often than not. As a result, transshipment may be necessary. If you allow transshipment, we would do our best to make further contacts with the forwarder. In this case, you must bear the additional charges.

Please take the above into consideration and let us know your decision as early as possible.

Sincerely,

Julie

 **Notes**

1. transshipment:*n.* 转运

e. g. ：Transshipment will be made at Hong Kong.

将在香港转船。

transship:*v.* 转运

e. g. ：The goods should be transshipped at Qingdao.

货物在青岛转运。

2. partial shipments:分批装运,指一个合同项下的货物分若干批或若干期装运

3. $5\times40'$ HQ:5 个 40 英尺高柜

4. comply with:依照,符合

e. g. ：Visitors to the factory must comply with the rules.

来工厂的访客必须遵守规章。

to comply with one's request/demand/wishes 满足某人的要求/愿望

5. in stock:库存货物

out of stock 无货　stock goods 库存货物

limited/low/heavy stock 有限的/少量的/充足的库存

e. g. ：Our stocks are running down/short/low.

我们的现货越来越少。

stock:*v.* 储备

e. g. ：We do not stock these goods.

我们不储备这些货。

stock up with 办货,进货

stock exchanges 股票交易所

6. liner service:班轮运输

tramp:不定期航线运输

7. bear:*v.* 负担

e. g. : Owing to your negligence, you have to bear the responsibility.

由于你方疏忽，你们不得不承担责任。

The extra expenses are to be borne by you.

额外的费用由你承担。

10.3 Writing Steps and Tips

The main contents of letters concerning shipment include: giving your purpose of writing; stating the specific way of shipment; expressing your hope that shipment will be made immediately according to the contract stipulations.

Based on the above specimen letters, some essential writing steps and tips about business letters on shipment can be clearly and accurately summed up into the following points.

Writing steps	Examples of expressions
(1)Identify reference 告知对方相关信息	We refer to Contract No. 1343 signed between us on August 1, 2014 for Men's Shirts, which stipulates that the latest shipment date is October 15, 2014.
(2) Confirm shipping details, such as name of goods, shipping schedule, shipping documents etc. 确认装运的相关细节	As contracted, the delivery time of this order is up to January 31, 2013.
(3)Express the reasons why punctual shipment is required 表明如期装运的必要性	As our company is in urgent need of the goods, we would like to emphasize again the importance of the punctual shipment within the validity of the L/C.
(4) Illustrate the consequences of the action 阐明无法如期装运的后果	In case you should fail to effect shipment by the end of this month, we would have to lodge a claim against you for the loss, as is stipulated in the sales confirmation.
(5)Indicate the writer's hope or expectation 表达期望	Please take the above into consideration and let us know your decision as early as possible.

10.4 Useful Expressions on Shipment

1. The Order No. 123 is so urgently requires that we have to ask you to speed up the shipment.

我们要急用第 123 号订单所订货物，请你们加快装船速度。

2. How long does it usually take you to make a delivery?

通常你方需要多长时间交货？

3. Shipment should be made before October, otherwise we are not able to catch the season.

十月前必须交货，否则就赶不上季节了。

4. We are terribly worried about late shipment.

我方非常担心货物迟交。

5. We have not yet received your shipment advice. Please let us know whether shipment has been effected.

我方至今未收到装船通知，请告知是否已经装船。

6. Please inform us of the date of shipment for contract No. 008.

请尽快通知我方第008号合同项下的货物的交货日期。

7. When is the earliest possible date you can ship the goods?

你们最早什么时候可以装运？

8. We trust that you will make all necessary arrangements to deliver the goods in time.

我们相信你方会及时做必要的装运安排。

9. Please be informed that the shipment of the cargo was sent yesterday, airway bill No. 123.

特此通知这批货物昨天已装运，航空货物的领取号码是 No.123。

10. We have to remind you that shipment of our order No. 12 is rapidly becoming overdue.

我们必须提醒你们，我方12号订单的货物的装运很快就要过期了。

11. In case you do not receive the goods on or before December 1, please let us know.

万一你方没有在12月1日或之前收到货物，请告知我方。

12. You may rest assured that we will ship the goods next week without delay.

请放心我们一定在下周装运货物。

13. Shipment must be made within the prescribed time limit, as further extension will not be considered.

装船期必须限于预订的日期，再次展期将不予考虑。

14. Your L/C has not reached us up to the present moment, which has involved us in no small difficulty.

你方信用证至今未到，这给我们造成不小的麻烦。

15. Since there are regular direct sailings between our two ends, we intend to transport the goods we ordered by sea.

既然我们两地之间有定期直达航班，所以希望海运我们的这批货。

16. We wish to advise you that your Order No. 79 has been shipped today.

兹通知你方79号订单下货物今天已装船。

17. We'd like to accept your proposal to change the unloading port to Los Angeles.

我们愿意接受你们的建议，把卸货港改为洛杉矶。

18. The duplicate shipping documents including bill of lading, invoice, packing list and inspection certificate were airmailed to you today.

包括提单、发票、装箱单和检验证书在内的装运单证副本今日航寄你处。

19. According to the terms stipulated in the contract, shipping the goods is to be made in three equal monthly installments.

根据合同规定的条款,这批货每月分三批等量装运。

20. We hope the goods will reach you in safety and come up to your expectation.

我们希望这批货物会安全抵达你方并符合你方的期望。

10.5 Exercises

Ⅰ. Multiple choices.

1. _____ your claim of April 10, we very much regret that...

   A. Refer to   B. Referring to   C. Refer   D. With references

2. We wish to _____ your attention _____ the fact that...

   A. call,to   B. make,to   C. put,in   D. get,with

3. Our customers are pressing us _____ ship the goods in time.

   A. to   B. for   C. that we   D. on

4. We have not received any news from them _____ the present moment.

   A. to   B. at   C. in   D. up to

5. In the meantime, please _____ us informed of developments at your end.

   A. keep   B. have   C. touch   D. fail

6. The goods are not _____ our satisfaction.

   A. for   B. in   C. to   D. of

7. It is important that shipment _____ before the end of this month.

   A. will be made   B. must be made   C. can be made   D. be made

8. We feel it our duty to remind you _____ this matter.

   A. by   B. of   C. for   D. in

9. We are obliged _____ you _____ your early reply.

   A. to,for   B. to,to   C. for,to   D. for,for

10. _____ no circumstances shall we disappoint a customer.

    A. On   B. In   C. Under   D. By

Ⅱ. Translate the following terms and expressions.

1. partial shipment   6. 即期交货

2. to make delivery of the goods   7. 装运期

3. shipping instruction   8. 两批等量装运

4. shipping advice   9. 货位

5. in good condition   10. 大致抵达时间

Ⅲ. Translate the following sentences into Chinese.

1. The order No. 134 is so urgently required that we have to ask you to speed up shipment.

2. As stipulated under the contract，the seller should cable the shipping advice to the buyer as soon as the goods are on board.

3. Such being the case，we'll have to make everything ready for the arrival of your vessel.

4. We prefer to ship whatever is ready instead of waiting for the completion of the entire lot.

5. We have expressly stated that the stipulations of the L/C should comply with the terms of the contract.

6. We will do our best to advance shipment but cannot commit ourselves.

7. The goods are being prepared for immediate delivery and will be ready for shipment tomorrow.

8. Please inform us 10 days prior to the shipment of the name of steamer，estimated time of arrival，loading capacity，contract number and forwarding agent.

9. We may see our way to advance time of shipment to July after checking the stocks.

10. If you can guarantee punctual delivery，we shall place large orders with you.

Ⅳ. Translate the following sentences into English.

1. 请尽快装运。

2. 我们相信你方会及时做必要的装运安排。

3. 请放心我们一定会在下周装运货物。

4. 你方信用证至今未到，这给我们造成了不小的麻烦。

5. 68 号合同项下的货物已于今天下午由"东风"轮装运。

6. 我们遗憾地获悉要延迟装运我方货物。

7. 6 月初是我们能够做到的最早交货日期。

8. 一般说来，我们在收到有关的信用证后三个月内可交货。

9. 根据合同规定的条款，这批货每月分三批等量装运。

10. 我们希望把上海定为装运港，因为它离货物产地比较近。

Ⅴ. Write a letter according to the following requirements.

1. 6 月 3 日要求提早装运第 521 号合约的来信收到。

2. 本公司联络了船运公司，得知 5 月 1 日前开往贵公司港口的船只已经没有剩余货位，因而不能提前装运，深感抱歉。

3. 然而，本公司可确保该货物将于合约指定的时间送抵。

 **Appendix 1 装货单**

中国外轮式代理公司
CHINA OCEAN SHIPPING AGENCY
装货单 SHIPPING ORDER

装单号码_____ 日期_____ 海关编号

S/O# _____ Date _____ Customs Ves. # _____

船名_____航次_____装往地点

S. S. _____ Voy. _____ Destination _____

搬运人

Shipper _____

收货人

Conaigiee _____

通知

Notify _____

标记及号码 Marks and Numbers	件数 Quantity	货名 Deseription of Goods	质量 Weight		尺码 Measures
			净重 Net	毛重 Gross	

合计　　　　　　　　　　　　　共重
Total　　　　　　　　　　　　　Total
合计
SAY

请将上述完好状况货物,予以装船,并希签署收货单为荷。

Please receive en boerd the above goods in good order and condition and sigh the accomanying receipt for same.

装入何舱

Stowed _____

实　　收

Received _____

理货员签名

Tallied By _____

代理人

As ugents _____

Appendix 2 大副收据

中国外轮式代理公司

CHINA OCEAN SHIPPING AGENCY

收货单

MATE'S RECEIPTS/O NO.

船　　名　　　　　　　　航次　　　　　　　　目的港

Vessel Name _____ Voy. _____ For _____

搬运人

Shipper _____

受货人

Consignee _____

通知

Nocify _____

下列完成状况之货物已收妥无损

The goods in the following completed condition have been kept intact

标记及号码 Marks and Numbers	件数 Quantity	货名 Deseription of Goods	毛重(千克) Gross weight（kg）	尺码(立方米) Measures(m³)

共计件数(大写)

Total Number of Packeges in Writing

日期　　　　　　　　时间

Date _____ Time _____

装入何舱

Stowed _____

实　　收

Received _____

理货员签名

Tallied By _____

大　　副

Chief Officer _____

Chapter 11　Claims and Settlements

Learning objectives

　　To know how to lodge a claim.

　　To know how to settle or decline a claim.

　　To grasp the key words and sentence patterns on claims.

　　To grasp the structure of writing a claim letter and a reply.

11.1　Brief Introduction

In international trade, disputes always arise between sellers and buyers for their different rights and duties, so that complaint, claim, arbitration, or even litigation shall happen. Complaints or claims may sometimes arise in spite of our well-planned and careful work in the performance of a contract. There are plenty of reasons for disputes between sellers and buyers, such as the quality not in compliance with the stipulations of a contract, the shortage of quantity or weight, the damage of the cargoes, improper packing, late delivery of cargoes and so on.

Some problems shall be borne by the sellers, some are attributed to the carriers' negligence, and some problems may be covered by insurance policy, so buyers can write letters to lodge claims against any relevant party.

Generally speaking, there are two kinds of complaints or claims being often made by buyers:

a. A genuine complaint or claim, which arises from one of the following situations:

• The wrong goods may have been sent.

• The quality may not be satisfactory.

• The goods may have been delivered damaged or late.

• The price charged may be excessive, or not as agreed.

b. A false complaint or claim, made by buyers who find faults with the goods as an excuse to escape from their contracts, either because they no longer want the goods or because they have found that they can get them cheaper elsewhere.

We must deal with complaints or claims in accordance with the principle of "on the first grounds, to our advantage and with restraint" and settle them amicably to the satisfaction of all parties concerned. The following rules should be followed by the seller when dealing with a complaint:

• The first thing that has to be decided is whether the complaint is justified. If it is so, the sellers have to admit it readily, express his or her regret and promise to solve the problems as soon as possible, such as replacing the goods, refund or make compensation for the losses.

• If the complaint or claim is not justified, you can point this out politely and agreeably, convince the other party and refuse the claim.

• If the seller cannot deal with a complaint promptly, acknowledge it at once; explain that the matter is being investigated and a full reply will be sent later.

The tone of complaint letters should not be aggressive or insulting, as this would annoy the readers and not encourage them to solve the problem.

11.2   Specimen Letters

 Letter 1   A complaint about late delivery

Dear Sirs,

On June 3 we placed our Order 725 with you for 50,000 lots No. 3A bolts and then thousand No. 35 screwdrivers.

Although your salesman assures us of three-week delivery on small orders, it is now six weeks since the order was placed. Some of these bolts are required by a customer to complete a shipment of furniture to South America. Your delay is causing great loss to him and the loss of considerable goodwill to us.

Please do everything possible to see that order is shipped to reach us no later than Monday, July 15th.

Very truly yours,

(signature)

 **Notes**

1. place an order with sb. for sth. : 向某人订购某货物

fill an order 交付订货   cancel an order 取消订单

e.g. : We've received an order for two tons of coal.

我们收到了订购两吨煤的订单。

2. bolt: 螺栓

3. screwdriver: 螺丝刀

4. assure sb. of sth. : 使某人对某事确信无疑

e.g. : They tried to assure him of their willingness to work.

他们试图向他保证他们愿意工作。

5. considerable: *adj.* 相当多的,相当大的

e.g. : It's considerably colder this morning.

今天早上冷得多了。

6. goodwill：*n.* 善意，友善，信誉

show goodwill towards sb. 向某人表达善意

e. g.：Given goodwill on both sides, I'm sure we can reach agreement.

鉴于双方都有善意，我相信我们能达成协议。

The goodwill is being sold together with the shop.

建立信誉和创企业商誉有密切的关系。

7. see that：(or see to it that) 务必，一定要注意到

e. g.：See to it that you're ready on time.

请贵方务必准时做好准备。

 Letter 2　A complaint about goods not corresponding to samples

Dear Sirs,

　　Attention：Customer Service Department

　　On February 9th I received an incorrect shipment of Widgets fulfilling the order I placed on February 3rd. Rather than the 300 Deluxe Yellow Widgets (Ref. ♯ XT111) that I ordered, the shipment contained 300 Regular Yellow Widgets (Ref. ♯ XT101).

　　As per the instructions we received on the telephone, the unwanted Regular Widgets were shipped back the same day. It was promised that the correct items would be shipped out the very next day, February 10th, and be delivered freight free the following week.

　　As of this date we have not yet received our shipment of Deluxe Widgets. This was a COD order, paid for with check ♯250564 in the amount of ＄1,913.50, which has already cleared through our bank. If these Widgets cannot be shipped February 20th, please cancel the order and send a refund check in the amount of ＄1,368.00 for the unfulfilled portion of the order.

　　I have enclosed a copy of the original order.

Thank you

 **Notes**

1. Customer Service Department：客户服务部

2. widget：*n.* 小机械，装饰物

3. deluxe：*adj.* 高质量的，豪华的

a deluxe hotel/car/bed 豪华旅馆/汽车/床

4. unwanted：*adj.* 不需要的；有害的；讨厌的；空闲的

unwanted pregnancy/goods 不需要的商品

e. g.：She felt unwanted.

她感到别人不需要她。

5. COD：abbr. (cash on delivery)货到付款

e. g.：It is very fair for us to do business with COD.

以货到付款的方式做生意对我们双方都是非常公平的。

6. clear：*v.* 通过

　e. g. ：Our baggage has cleared customs.

　　　　我们的行李通过海关检查。

7. enclose：*v.* 把某物放入信封、包裹等中

　e. g. ：I have enclosed a cheque for ＄100.

　　　　我已附上一张 100 美元的支票。

8. unfulfilled：*adj.* 未实现的，未得到满足的

　e. g. ：Do you have any unfulfilled ambitions?

　　　　你有未实现的抱负吗?

 Letter 3　A complaint about the shortage of quantity

Dear Mr. Choi,

　　　　　　　　　　　Re. Order No. 768197

　　I am writing to inform you that the goods we ordered from your company have not been supplied correctly.

　　On 24 June 2016 we placed an order with your firm for 12,000 ultra-super long-life batteries. The consignment arrived yesterday but contained only 1,200 batteries.

　　This error put our firm in a difficult position, as we had to make some emergency purchases to fulfill our commitments to all our customers. This caused us considerable inconvenience.

　　I am writing to ask you to make up the shortfall immediately and to ensure that such errors do not happen again. Otherwise, we may have to look elsewhere for our supplies.

　　I look forward to hearing from you by return.

　　　　　　　　　　　　　　　　　　　　Yours sincerely,

　　　　　　　　　　　　　　　　　　　　(signature)

 **Notes**

1. consignment：*n.* 货物

2. commitment：*n.* 承诺，献身（～to sth. /to do sth.）

　e. g：We made a commitment to keep working together.

　　　　我们承诺继续一起工作。

　　　　We're looking for someone with a real sense of commitment to the job.

　　　　我们在寻求对此工作真正能尽职尽责的人。

3. shortfall：*n.* 差额，不足，赤字（～in sth.）

　e. g：a shortfall in the annual budget 年度预算的不足

4. ensure：*v.* 保证，使某人一定得到

　e. g：The book ensured his success.

　　　　这本书保证了他的成功。

These pills should ensure you a good night's sleep.

这些药片可以保证你睡个好觉。

 Letter 4   A complaint against the carrier

Dear Sirs,

We have just received some information from Messrs. Bombay & Sons in Colombo, the consignee under B/L No. 100 dated October 11, that two of the 100 cases shipped from Guangzhou to Paris per S/S "peace" are missing. The consignee contacted your agents (of shipping company) in Colombo about it and they were advised to get in touch with us direct to inquire into the matter. As matters stand, it is legibly indicated in the B/L, shipped in apparently good order a condition. The same indication appears in our shipping order and your Mate's Receipt.

It is therefore obvious that shortage is due to your fault, and we hereby notify you that we reserve the right to claim on you for the shortage, should it be subsequently confirmed. Your early clarification and settlement of the case will be appreciated.

Yours faithfully,

(signature)

 **Notes**

1. Colombo：*n.* 科伦坡（斯里兰卡首都）

2. as matters stand：照目前的情况

e. g.：As matters now stand, there is no way out of the trouble.

在目前的情形之下，没有解决困难的方法。

3. legible：*adj.* （指印刷或字迹）清楚的

e. g.：The inscription is still legible.

碑文仍清晰可见。

Please write more legibly.

请写得更清晰一些。

4. Shipping Order：装货单

5. Mate's Receipt：大幅收据，又称收货单

6. hereby：*adv.* 据此，特此

e. g.：We hereby heartily endorse the framework laid out by the Bowles-Simpson Commission.

我们在此衷心赞同鲍尔斯·辛普森委员会提出的框架。

7. subsequently：*adv.* 随后，其后；后来

e. g.：They subsequently heard he had left the country.

他们后来听说他已离开了那个国家。

8. clarification：*n.* 澄清，被澄清

e. g.：The whole issue needs clarification.

整件事情都需要澄清。

 Letter 5   A complaint concerning damaged goods

Dear Sirs,

Our order No. U23

The 100 Coffee Sets supplied to the above order were delivered yesterday, but we regret that 18 sets were badly damaged.

The packages containing the coffee sets appeared to be in good condition and we accepted and signed for them without question. We unpacked the coffee sets with great care and can only assume that the damage must be due to careless handling at some stage prior to packing.

We shall be glad if you will replace all 15 sets as soon as you can. Meanwhile, we have put the damaged coffee sets aside in case you need them to support a claim on your suppliers for compensation.

Yours sincerely,

(signature)

 **Notes**

1. The 100 Coffee Sets supplied to the above order were delivered. 上述订单中所订 100 台咖啡机已交付。

2. We regret that 18 sets were badly damaged. 我方遗憾地表示 18 台已被严重损坏。

3. in good condition：完好

4. unpack. . . with great care：小心打开……包装

5. assume：推断、假定

6. The damage must be due to careless handling. 损坏是粗鲁处理方式造成的。

7. put. . . sets aside：把……放在一边、留着……备用

8. Support a claim on your suppliers for compensation. 向贵方的供应商提出索赔。

 **Letter 6   The reply**

Dear Sirs,

Your order No. U23

We are sorry to learn from your letter of the 5th that some of the coffee sets supplied to the above order were damaged when they reached you. We will certainly replace them and have in fact instructed our Beijing Branch to send them by parcel post.

We regret the need for you to write to us and will do our best to improve our methods of handling so as to avoid further inconvenience to any customer. It will not be necessary for you to keep the damaged coffee sets and they can be destroyed.

Yours sincerely,

(signature)

 **Notes**

1. We are sorry to learn from your letter of... that... : 我方从贵方……月……日来函中遗憾获悉……

2. We will certainly replace them and have in fact instructed our Beijing Branch to send them by parcel post. 我方定会更换产品,实际上我方已经通知我公司北京分部邮寄更换的产品了。

3. improve our methods of handling: 改进我方的处理方式

4. further inconvenience: 更多或更大的不便之处

11.3   Writing Steps and Tips

Based on the above specimen letters, some essential writing steps and tips about business letters on claims or complaints can be clearly and accurately summed up into the following points.

1. A Letter of claim or Complaint(提出索赔的信函)

Writing steps	Examples of expressions
(1)Regretting the need to complain about the goods 对货物提出索赔,并表示遗憾	We regret/are sorry to say that... We regret to have to complain about... Much to our regret,...
(2)Stating your reasons for such complaint and the inconvenience caused 说明要求索赔的原因和由此而造成的不便	We have received a few complaints from customers about... We have just received the survey report from... certifying that... The inferior quality of... causes us considerable difficulty and it is hard for us to dispose of it.
(3)Suggesting how the matter should be put right 提出解决索赔的建议、办法或要求	Based on the survey report, we hereby register our claim for... in all. We would like you to refund the money we have paid you for... We have to lodge a claim against you for...
(4)Hoping to get the immediate treatment 表示希望对方及时解决或告知处理办法	We hope this matter will come to your best attention. We are awaiting your prompt reply. We trust you will promptly settle this claim.

2. A Letter of Replying to a Claim or Complaint a settlement（回复索赔-理赔的信函）

Writing steps	Examples of expressions
(1)Regretting the claim or complaint about the goods 对该索赔事件表示遗憾	We regret/are sorry that we hear... We regret to learn about... Much to our regret, we heard that...
(2)Stating the results for such claim or complaint after the investigation 说明调查的结果	Based on the immediate investigation we made, we find that... After looking into the matter in details, so far we have not found that...
(3)Stating how to settle the claim or complaint 表示将如何解决索赔	We prepare to compensate you by 20% of the total invoice value. We regret for the losses you have suffered and agree to compensate you by... We regret we cannot entertain your claim, which is without any foundation.

11.4   Useful Expressions on Claims and Settlements

1. We have received claims from our customers, and as a result, we have to request that you compensate us for the loss.

我方已经收到了客户的索赔,因此,我们不得不要求贵方赔偿我们的损失。

2. On examination we find that the consignment does not correspond with the original sample.

检查后我方发现这批货与原来的样品不一样。

3. Your shipment of our S/C No. 955 has been found short-weight by 200kgs.

现发现贵方所发运的我方 955 号销售合同的货物短重 200 千克。

4. We reserve the right to claim compensation from you for any damage.

我方保留对任何损失向贵方提出索赔的权利。

5. We regret for the losses you have suffered and agree to compensate you by GBP 15,500.00.

对贵方所遭受的损失我方深表遗憾,同意赔偿 15500.00 英镑。

6. In view of our friendly business relations, we prepare to meet your claim for the short weight of 20 M/T.

鉴于我们的友好业务关系,我方准备接受贵方短重 20 公吨的索赔要求。

7. We should lodge a claim for all the losses incurred as a consequence of your failure to ship our order in time.

由于贵方未能及时装运我方订单,我方将对所发生的一切损失提出索赔。

8. As requested, we will send you a replacement within a week and hope you will be

pleased with the new lot.

根据要求,我们将在一周内给贵方更换,希望贵方对新产品满意。

9. I propose we compensate you by 5% of the total amount of the contract.

我建议我们赔偿贵方合同总金额的 5%。

10. Any complaint about the quality of the products should be lodged within 30 days after their arrival.

任何关于产品质量的投诉应在其到达后 30 天内提出。

11. We regret our inability to accommodate your claim.

我们很遗憾不能接受贵方的索赔。

12. We regret that your claim on shortage cannot be accepted.

很遗憾,贵方关于短缺的索赔不能被接受。

13. Let us assure you that we shall take every care and such an accident like this should never occur again.

我方向贵方保证,我们将精心处理每一步骤,这样的事故永远不会再发生。

14. As it is a matter concerning the insurance, we hope that you will refer the claim to the insurance company or their agent at your end.

由于这是一个有关保险的问题,我方希望贵方向当地的保险公司或其代理人提出索赔。

15. Since the dispute cannot be settled through negotiation, we agree to settle it by arbitration.

由于争议无法通过谈判解决,我方同意通过仲裁解决。

11.5 Exercises

Ⅰ. Translate the following sentences into Chinese.

1. We enclose two copies of Survey Report together with our Statement of Claim which amounts to US＄100,000.

2. As the whole parcel is of no use to us, we must ask you to refund us the invoice value and the inspection fee as per the statement of claim enclosed.

3. Enclosed is a check for USD 500, which will cover the whole loss of yours.

4. We have received your remittance in settlement of our claim.

5. We are immediately sending replacements of those damaged tea sets.

6. As our shipping documents can confirm that the goods were in perfect condition when they left here, and that evidently show they were damaged in transportation. Therefore, we cannot give our consideration to your claim.

Ⅱ. Translate the following sentences into English.

1. 我方想说明这些棉布在装运前经过仔细的检查,并与合同中的规定完全一致。鉴于此情况,我方不打算接受你方的索赔。

2. 按确认书规定,该批茶具应以适合远洋运输的坚固木箱包装,为此,我只好要你方负责这次损坏事故,并向你方索赔由此遭受的损失。

3. 你方索赔不予受理,因为它是在货物抵达目的地 30 天后提出的。

4. 鉴于货物质量比要求低得多,我们要求对低质量进行价值 1000 美元的索赔。

5. 我方随函附上检验证书副本以及金额为 20000 美元的索赔清单。

6. 我方对上批船货的全部损失向你方提出 5000 美元的索赔。

Ⅲ. Write a letter according to the information given in the following situations.

Suppose your company has just received 70 sets of automatic alarms, which you order for 75 sets. Make a claim against the supplier, Sunshine Machine Works, on the shortage of the machines.

References

1. R Holt, N Sampson. International Business Correspondence Handbook [M]. Beijing：Foreign Language Teaching and Research Press, 1999.

2. Alan Bond. 英文商务信函模板通[M]. 苏海霞，译. 北京：机械工业出版社, 2010.

3. 艾湘华. 英语文体写作一本就够用[M]. 北京：科学出版社, 2011.

4. 董晓波. 国际商务信函写作[M]. 北京：对外经济贸易大学出版社, 2013.

5. 董金玲，郝景亚，郑凌霄. 国际商务函电双语教程[M]. 北京：机械工业出版社, 2011.

6. 耿民. 商务英语函电[M]. 北京：对外经济贸易大学出版社, 2012.

7. 浩瀚，陈淑萍. 商务英语写作实战实例[M]. 北京：北京航空航天大学出版社, 2011.

8. 焦微玲. 外贸英语函电——从基础到实践[M]. 北京：电子工业出版社, 2013.

9. 金哲虎. 国际商务函电[M]. 北京：北京大学出版社, 2013.

10. 喆儒. 现代国际商务函电[M]. 北京：人民邮电出版社, 2011.

11. 罗凤翔，杜清萍. 国际商务英语模拟实训教程[M]. 北京：中国商务出版社, 2005.

12. 廖瑛，张春敏. 实用外贸英语函电教程[M]. 北京：对外经济贸易大学出版社, 2016.

13. 林染. E时代双语商务书信[M]. 北京：海潮出版社, 2010.

14. 李蕾. 商务英语函电[M]. 北京：对外经济贸易大学出版社, 2011.

15. 林涛，姜丽. 国际商务英文与函电[M]. 北京：清华大学出版社, 2011.

16. 李文彪. 国际贸易函电[M]. 北京：对外经济贸易大学出版社, 2016.

17. 聂春阁，王阳. 外贸函电及流程[M]. 北京：中国商务出版社, 2013.

18. 凌华倍，朱佩芳. 外经贸英语函电与谈判[M]. 3版. 北京：中国对外经济贸易出版社, 2004.

19. 陆墨珠. 国际商务函电[M]. 5版. 北京：中国商务出版社, 2006.

20. 芮燕萍. 领先商务英语函电. 北京：高等教育出版社, 2013.

21. 滕美荣，徐楠. 外贸英语函电[M]. 北京：首都经济贸易大学出版社, 2005.

22. 田野青，郭蕊. 国际贸易英文函电[M]. 北京：机械工业出版社, 2010.

23. 檀文茹. 商务英语函电[M]. 2版. 北京：对外经济贸易大学出版社, 2016.

24. 王乃彦. 对外经贸英语函电[M]. 4版. 北京：对外经济贸易大学出版社, 2009.

25. 杨晋. 当代国际商务函电[M]. 天津：天津大学出版社, 2011.

26. 吴雯. 国际商务英语函电[M]. 2版. 北京：对外经济贸易大学出版社, 2015.

27. 隋思忠. 外贸英语函电[M]. 大连：东北财经大学出版社, 2010.

28. 殷秀玲. 外贸函电[M]. 北京：立信会计出版社, 2011.

29. 曾勇民. 国际商务函电[M]. 北京：北京理工大学出版社, 2011.

30. 赵银德. 外贸函电[M]. 北京：机械工业出版社, 2007.

31. 周宁. 物流英语[M]. 2版. 北京：电子工业出版社, 2012.